T0089394

# W. B. YEATS

# THE WINDING STAIR AND OTHER POEMS (1933)

## A FACSIMILE EDITION

WITH AN INTRODUCTION AND NOTES

BY

### GEORGE BORNSTEIN

SCRIBNER

NEW YORK   LONDON   TORONTO   SYDNEY

SCRIBNER
A Division of Simon & Schuster, Inc.
1230 Avenue of the Americas
New York, NY 10020

First Scribner trade paperback edition March 2011

For information about special discounts for bulk purchases,
please contact Simon & Schuster Special Sales at 1-866-506-1949
or business@simonandschuster.com.

The Simon & Schuster Speakers Bureau can bring authors to your live event.
For more information or to book an event contact the Simon & Schuster Speakers
Bureau at 1-866-248-3049 or visit our website at www.simonspeakers.com.

DESIGNED BY ERICH HOBBING

Manufactured in the United States of America

5   7   9   10   8   6   4

Library of Congress Control Number: 2010033779

ISBN 978-1-4165-8992-1

# CONTENTS

# PREFACE

This edition offers a facsimile of the first London edition of *The Winding Stair and Other Poems,* published in London by Macmillan on 19 September 1933. The copy used is that in the Special Collections Library, University of Michigan, Ann Arbor. The present edition adds an introduction tracing the assembly and design of the 1933 volume as well as annotations to that edition, including editorial notes on the poems.

I am grateful to the late Richard Finneran of the University of Tennessee and to Samantha Martin of Scribner for suggesting and supporting this project with advice and encouragement. I am also grateful to the splendid librarians at the University of Michigan, in particular Peggy Daub, Kathy Beame, Barbara MacAdam, and Judy Avery. Nate Mills and Jessica Morton served as capable research assistants. It is also a pleasure to acknowledge support from the University of Michigan for the early stages of the project and from the Andrew W. Mellon Foundation for the later ones.

This edition is dedicated to the memory of Richard J. and Mary FitzGerald Finneran, in Yeats's phrase "friends who have been friends indeed," and to Nora FitzGerald and Rich and Kate Finneran.

# ABBREVIATIONS OF WORKS
# BY W. B. YEATS

**EE**  *Early Essays*, vol. 4 of The Collected Works of W. B. Yeats, ed. Richard J. Finneran and George Bornstein (New York: Scribner, 2007)

**L**  *Letters of W. B. Yeats*, ed. Allan Wade (New York: Macmillan, 1955)

**LE**  *Later Essays*, vol. 5 of The Collected Works of W. B. Yeats, ed. William H. O'Donnell with assistance from Elizabeth Bergmann Loizeaux (New York: Scribner, 1994)

**LTSM**  *W. B. Yeats and T. Sturge Moore: Their Correspondence 1901–1937*, ed. Ursula Bridge (London: Routledge & Kegan Paul, 1953)

# INTRODUCTION:
# THE DESIGN OF YEATS'S
# *THE WINDING STAIR AND*
# *OTHER POEMS*

*The Winding Stair and Other Poems* is Yeats's longest separate volume of verse. It includes sixty-four different poems (by contrast, the preceding volume, *The Tower,* has only thirty-six), among them such Yeatsian masterpieces as "A Dialogue of Self and Soul," "Byzantium," the Coole Park poems, "Vacillation," and two separately titled long sequences ending with the exquisite lyric "From the 'Antigone.'" Because that length renders a poem-by-poem commentary unfeasible here, I focus instead on the *design* of the volume, meaning first its symbolic cover, on which Yeats collaborated with his friend and favorite book designer, T. Sturge Moore, and then the revealing overall arrangement of poems within the resultant book. But first, a word about reading Yeats's poetry beyond the obvious and customary focus on verse form on the one hand and thematic concerns (history, biography, gender, philosophy, and the like) on the other.

As Hugh Kenner pointed out early on, Yeats did not simply write poems, he wrote books of poems. Yeats famously invoked in "Adam's Curse" the time he spent "stitching and unstitching" the lines. He also spent considerable time stitching and unstitching the poems to each other. The surviving manuscripts sport masses of alternate lists of orderings for his various volumes, and he often re-revised those orderings for subsequent editions. He did the same thing for collected editions of his work at various times throughout his life. There are even two alternate orderings for his collected poems as a whole, both approved by him at different moments during the 1930s. Partisans of one or the other ordering often claim that their preferred arrangement is the true one, but the important point seems the very existence of alternate placements sanctioned by the poet himself. Within each volume, the first thing to note is that the arrangement of poems is never chronological by date of composition. Yeats strove to make that clear even to those of us who are not advanced textual scholars, for example by the dates he sometimes supplied for his individual poems. Thus, he dated the first four poems of *The Tower* volume in this way: "Sailing to Byzantium" 1927, "The Tower" lyric 1926, "Meditations in Time of Civil War" 1923, and, of course, "Nineteen Hundred and Nineteen" in the title year. In the case of *The Winding Stair and Other Poems*, Yeats not only composed the opening "In Memory of Eva Gore-Booth and Con Markiewicz" and closing "From the 'Antigone'" at nearly the same time but even used the same manuscript pages for some of the drafts. So if the ordering is not chronological, what is it? It is usually both thematic and formal instead, and often displays a dynamically developing argument in which poems interact with and "correct" each other. Hostile critics of Yeats often fail to notice that the poems they like to critique most, such as "The Gyres" or "Under Ben Bulben," *open* volumes whose subsequent contents critique them more fully than the critics themselves do, as the poems move downward upon life and upon more human and humane concerns.

*The Winding Stair* (1933) appeared relatively late in Yeats's life, when he was sixty-eight. One of the great things about reading Yeats is that one sees different things at different ages. When I first encountered him at seventeen, for example, I found that the line "I thought it all out twenty years ago" expressed a fabulous, almost mythological amount of time. Now, as the country singer Waylon Jennings reminds us, I would say to that seventeen-year-old self, "I've got heartaches older than you." Reading him at sixty-eight, I find myself drawn repeatedly to those poems about overall patterns of life, history, and personal experience. The volume itself puts together (with some rearrangement) two separate earlier books of Yeats—*The Winding Stair* (1929) and *Words for Music Perhaps* (1932), both published by small, fine printing presses. The first, *The Winding Stair* (1929) from Fountain Press in New York, included the first five poems of the later *Winding Stair* volume and then the concluding sequence "A Woman Young and Old." The second, *Words for Music Perhaps*, contained the rest of the final volume except for "Crazy Jane Talks with the Bishop." Yeats rearranged the contents considerably when he placed "Words for Music Perhaps" between the first five poems and the concluding sequence of the original *Winding Stair* volume, including moving the opening poem,

"Byzantium," to later in the book. He thus reprinted neither of the two main components of the final *Winding Stair* volume in their original order, but instead divided the 1929 volume into two parts and placed the rearranged "Words for Music Perhaps" between them. Further, adding the phrase "*and Other Poems*" to the title differentiated it from most of the other volumes of collected poems, with titles like *The Wind Among the Reeds, Responsibilities,* and *Michael Robartes and the Dancer.* "*And Other Poems*" suggested that perhaps this grouping made not quite as tight a unity as most others, though it does display wonderful architectonics of its own.

To begin with, *The Winding Stair and Other Poems* forms a near diptych with the preceding *Tower* volume. Yeats's own tower at Ballylee dominates both books; indeed, the title "The Winding Stair" itself refers to the spiral staircase inside Yeats's renovated Norman tower. The pairing carries over to individual poems as well: for example, *The Tower* opens with "Sailing to Byzantium" while *The Winding Stair* offers its companion piece "Byzantium," which itself opened the *Words for Music Perhaps* volume. And *The Tower* contains the eleven-poem sequence "A Man Young and Old," which ends with the brief lyric "From 'Oedipus at Colonus,'" while *The Winding Stair* contains its companion eleven-poem sequence "A Woman Young and Old," which ends with the lyric "From the 'Antigone.'" Even the word "winding" in the title echoes the last word of the *Tower* volume, "wound."

The linkage carries over to the cover designs, too, both of them symbolic renderings by the same artist,

T. Sturge Moore. Yeats repeatedly arranged for Moore to do covers for his work and corresponded with him about components of the design. The cover for this volume and its twin, *The Tower,* display paired geometric designs. The one for *The Tower* features Yeats's Norman tower at Ballylee along with the cottages at its base and the river that flows past it and reflects the scene, in accord with one of Yeats's favorite Hermetic adages, "as above, so below." The design thus calls attention to the philosophic, geographic, and historical underpinning of the volume, and through the tower structure its ties to Yeats's artistic and personal life as well. "I like to think of that building as a permanent symbol of my work," wrote Yeats to Moore. "As you know, all my art theories depend upon just this—rooting of mythology in the earth" (LTSM 114). Moore wrote back, "I think that the Tower is recognizably your Tower and not anyone else's." And of course Moore's cover highlights the major poem "The Tower" as well as the use of that image throughout the volume. Correspondingly, the winding staircase of the present volume highlights that feature of the tower along with its symbolic overtones, such as the gyres that Yeats saw patterning both history and personal experience. The design features, too, the fire that flickers throughout the volume, most notably in those "Flames that no faggot feeds, nor steel has lit, / Nor storm disturbs, flames begotten of flame" in "Byzantium." The same poem supplied the cock at the top left and the dolphin carrying a human being at the bottom center. Moore had written Yeats to inquire, "Is your dolphin to be so large that the whole of humanity can ride on its back?" to which Yeats pithily responded, "One dolphin, one man," and that is what the resultant design shows (LTSM 164–65; see p.xxxv of the present edition).

Yeats invokes the flames on Moore's symbolic cover first in the opening poem of the volume, his elegy "In Memory of Eva Gore-Booth and Con Markiewicz." Mindful of the impossibility of exploring everything in the volume, I stress here that opening poem, the key middle ones on Coole Park, and the successive alternate endings to the volume formed by "Stream and Sun at Glendalough," "The Delphic Oracle upon Plotinus," and finally the chorus "From the 'Antigone.'" Note that the opening, middle, and closing poems are all about women. In the opening one, Eva Gore-Booth and Con Markiewicz were, of course, the daughters of the Sir Henry Gore-Booth family, which owned Lissadell House, near Sligo in the West of Ireland. Eva (the "gazelle" in the poem) grew up to become, improbably, a labor organizer, mystic, and writer, while Constance (who had been presented as a debutante at the court of Queen Victoria) became a famous Irish nationalist leader, imprisoned for her part in the Easter Rising of 1916, and later a worker among the poor in Dublin, with more than 100,000 people attending her funeral. Both had recently passed away when Yeats composed his elegy. He divided it into two parts marked by a space break.

The first section focuses on the two Gore-Booths as girls or young women and has an intimate relation to the quatrain form rhyming *abba*, which runs through the entire poem. Here is the first section:

> The light of evening, Lissadell,
> Great windows open to the south,
> Two girls in silk kimonos, both
> Beautiful, one a gazelle.
> But a raving autumn shears
> Blossom from the summer's wreath;
> The older is condemned to death,
> Pardoned, drags out lonely years
> Conspiring among the ignorant.
> I know not what the younger dreams—
> Some vague Utopia—and she seems,
> When withered old and skeleton-gaunt,
> An image of such politics.
> Many a time I think to seek
> One or the other out and speak
> Of that old Georgian mansion, mix
> Pictures of the mind, recall
> That table and the talk of youth,
> Two girls in silk kimonos, both
> Beautiful, one a gazelle.

The first quatrain presents itself as a stable form depicting the two girls at the great house of Lissadell in their youthful grace and ending with a full stop at quatrain's end. However, the "But" opening the second quatrain signals a thematic change echoed by a formal one. From here on, the lives of the two girls go awry (at least, from the speaker's perspective), as the mad overtones of the word "raving" suggest. They commit themselves to abstract political causes, and both they and the image of Ireland they project become "withered old and skeleton-gaunt, / An image of such politics." Ireland, of course, is traditionally depicted as a woman (whether Cathleen ni Houlihan, the Shan Van Vocht, or another representation), and the first surviving draft of the poem applies the crone image to that country rather than to Eva and Con: "But Ireland is a hag," it reads. The remaining seven lines of the first section shift attention to the speaker and his desire to visit the sisters, mix pictures of the mind, and above all to "speak"; its last two lines repeat the last two lines of the first quatrain verbatim. Not only does the sense reach a maximum tension with the expected divisions of rhyme, but the unusually late placement of the caesura before the end words "mix" and "recall" further destabilizes expected patterns. Notice, too, how the quatrains act out formally the notion of an opening gone awry that the poem presents biographically. After the first quatrain, no other stops at the end of a perfect four lines of rhyme. Instead, the poem continually itself goes awry against its quatrain form: the second one syntactically spills over into five lines, reaching an end stop only at the end of the fifth line with the important word "ignorant." The rhyme scheme of the next quatrain begins with that line, but its syntax continues on through the first line of the next quatrain ("An image of such politics") before reaching a new end stop. Following that, the last seven lines all run into each other until the word "gazelle" ending line 20 and the first section of the poem. In one of Yeats's continual and amazing feats of versecraft, then, his manipulation of the verse acts out formally the thematic notion expressed in the lines semantically.

The second section focuses even more on the speaker. The sisters have now become "dear shadows" because they have recently passed away and so freed themselves from their great enemy, time, which in the speaker's view so disfigured them. In temporary despair, he imagines striking a match to burn up and so purify things of this world. Significantly, as he does so often— and it's a part of Yeats that makes me sometimes trust and even love him—Yeats includes himself among the misguided. "*We* the great gazebo built," he declares in abolition of a distinction between himself and the sisters on this point. Not just they but also he went astray; indeed, the manuscript draft puts it even more strongly: "*I* the great gazebo built," it reads, with Yeats's always shaky spelling rendering "gazebo" as "gazabo," suggesting that he pronounced it *gaz*-a-bo. A gazebo, of course, can be a summer structure in a yard or garden, a place to look from, and also in Anglo-Irish usage can refer to making yourself into a gazebo or object of ridicule. And nowadays one cannot avoid thinking of the contemporary poet Paul Muldoon's delicious parody in "7, Middagh Street," "Two girls, both beautiful, one a gazebo." In any case, it humanizes Yeats to see his most stringent criticism directed at himself rather than at others. That fire kindled at the end of "In Memory of Eva Gore-Booth and Con Markiewicz" runs not only through time but through the rest of the volume, including the fires of "Byzantium" and the "brand, or flaming breath" and tree that is half flame of "Vacillation." I pause next over the three Coole Park poems in the middle of the volume (if we exempt the two final sequences), and particularly over "Coole Park, 1929," in relation to the overall design of this book.

Coole Park was the home of Lady Gregory, Yeats's patron and friend. Lack of funds had forced her to sell it to the government in 1927, while she lived on there as tenant until her death in 1932, the year before *The Winding Stair and Other Poems* was published. In contrast to the Gore-Booth girls of the opening poem, here was a woman who brought out the best in her own heritage, again associated with a house that she fought to preserve (she was inevitably defeated, and the materials scandalously sold for scrap after her death, but at least she fought). Further, she succeeded in embodying her ideal in history and the actual world. Significantly, the poem is entitled "Coole Park, 1929" but could just as easily be called "Lady Gregory, 1929." Fond as he was of eight-line stanzas in his maturity, Yeats chose here ottava rima, an octave borrowed from the Italian and rhyming *abababcc* in iambic pentameter. Most famously used in English as the comic stanza of Byron's *Don Juan,* which rhymed "Aristotle" with "bottle," for example, Yeats turned it to serious purposes and his powerful mature syntax. He did that partly by his characteristic device of making syntax and stanza coincide. Looking back to his romantic roots, he explained in "A General Introduction for My Work," "I discovered some twenty years ago that I must seek, not as Wordsworth thought, words in common use, but a powerful and passionate syntax, and a complete coincidence between period and stanza" (*LE* 212). Notice how that works in the first stanza, where the poet meditates the evening landscape at Coole in a stanza consisting of a single sentence:

> I meditate upon a swallow's flight,
> Upon an aged woman and her house,
> A sycamore and lime tree lost in night
> Although that western cloud is luminous,
> Great works constructed there in nature's spite
> For scholars and for poets after us,
> Thoughts long knitted into a single thought,
> A dance-like glory that those walls begot.

The aged woman is, of course, Lady Gregory, and the western cloud is luminous as both she and Coole Park are at the end of their lives. Yeats loved the maxim "Art is art because it is not nature" (which he misattributed to Goethe, *EE* 371) and used it to describe Lady Gregory's achievement. She had made Coole a cultural and artistic center, enabling great works to be constructed there both *to spite* nature and *in spite* of nature. The stanza closes with one of Yeats's characteristic images of Unity of Being, the dance, as does "Among School Children" in the previous volume.

The middle two stanzas of the poem shift to past tense as Yeats first invokes for a stanza five of those who labored at Coole and then devotes the entire following stanza to Lady Gregory herself. The five are Douglas Hyde (president of the Gaelic League and later of Ireland), Yeats himself as "one that ruffled in a manly pose," the playwright John Synge, and Lady Gregory's two nephews—the nationalist John Shawe-Taylor who, retiring after the Boer War, devoted himself particularly to land reform, and the art critic, dealer, and administrator Hugh Lane who, in a controversial gesture, left his valuable collection to the city of Dublin if it would build an art gallery to house it (you can see the collection there to this day). Yeats sees Lady Gregory as not only organizing the five into formation, but creating a pattern that seemed to "whirl," a word that evokes both Yeats's historical gyres and the "winding" stair of the volume's title. Thanks to that, Coole becomes an opposing image to the Gore-Booths and to the gazebo that drove the poet to despair in the book's opening poem.

With the fourth and final stanza, Yeats shifts mental gears again. This time he neither contemplates a present Coole nor remembers a past one but instead returns briefly to the present for a line and then imagines a future Coole:

> Here, traveller, scholar, poet, take your stand
> When all those rooms and passages are gone,
> When nettles wave upon a shapeless mound
> And saplings root among the broken stone,
> And dedicate—eyes bent upon the ground,
> Back turned upon the brightness of the sun
> And all the sensuality of the shade—
> A moment's memory to that laurelled head.

He foresees a ruined Coole, such as shortly came to pass, which is why we cannot visit the house today, though we can visit the surviving site and woods. Yeats urges us to "take your stand" like soldiers and to honor Lady Gregory. The image combines his customary opposites, or "antinomies" as he called them, in this case especially sun and shade. The intensity of the emotion nearly breaks the ottava rima, as the syntax runs on from the final *b* rhyme into the first line of the couplet, resulting in the second line of the concluding couplet (the one that invokes Lady Gregory) seeming to stand alone. But besides its ottava rima form, the poem has a second one, closely linked to Romanticism. Its mental action, from meditating a present landscape to remembering or imagining a past or future one (Yeats does both here) and returning to the present, follows the structure of a greater Romantic lyric, a form invented by Wordsworth and Coleridge in poems like "Tintern Abbey," "Frost at Midnight," or "The Aeolian Harp" but also practiced by the second generation of Romantic poets, especially Keats in famous lyrics such as "Ode to a Nightingale" or (with artwork substituted for landscape) "Ode on a Grecian Urn." In that way, the poem itself enacts its own homage to Coole Park, displaying the sort of imaginative power and patterning that Lady Gregory had inspired there and that the poem itself represents. Just as "Romantic Ireland" was not really "dead and gone" in "September 1913" because it lived on in the voice of nationalist leader John O'Leary's most famous disciple, Yeats himself, so will Coole not really be gone because its creative power lives on in the poem itself and in the voice that speaks the poem. It is one more way in which during the following poem, "Coole and Ballylee, 1931," Yeats could famously claim of himself, Lady Gregory, and Synge, "We were the last romantics."

The third Coole Park poem in the volume, the slighter "For Anne Gregory," also focuses on a young woman, but this time in a comic way. Anne, who grew up at Coole, was the daughter of Major Robert Gregory and hence granddaughter of Lady Gregory. With splendid blond hair, she served as inspiration for Yeats's tribute to her, in which first a Yeats-like older male speaks, then a girl like Anne, and then the first speaker again. As usual, Yeats makes stanza and syntax coincide, with each stanza formed from a single sentence:

> 'Never shall a young man,
> Thrown into despair
> By those great honey-coloured
> Ramparts at your ear,
> Love you for yourself alone
> And not your yellow hair.'

> 'But I can get a hair-dye
> And set such colour there,
> Brown, or black, or carrot,
> That young men in despair
> May love me for myself alone
> And not my yellow hair.'

> 'I heard an old religious man
> But yesternight declare
> That he had found a text to prove

That only God, my dear,
Could love you for yourself alone
And not your yellow hair.'

In reading Yeats's many poems about women in this volume, one sometimes wonders what the women themselves would say back to the poet. In the case of this poem, we know, for Anne Gregory did provide a retrospective account in her charming brief memoir *Me and Nu: Childhood at Coole.* Here is how she recalled Yeats's recital of the poem during one of his extended stays at Coole Park when she herself was a teenager:

Some time after this W. B. Yeats wrote a poem for me alone, and again I wasn't entirely pleased to start with. I felt it was very doggerelly and not as romantic as I would have liked.

Mr. Yeats sent a message for me to go up to his sitting-room, and then said that he had written a poem called "Yellow Hair" and that he had dedicated it to me, and proceeded to read it, in his "humming" voice. We used to hear his voice "humming" away for hours while he wrote his verse. He used to hum the rhythm of a verse before he wrote the words, Grandma told us, and that was why his poems are so good to read aloud . . . but on this occasion I was petrified. I had no idea that he was going to write a poem to me, and had no idea at all what one should say when he had read it aloud.

It was agony! For once, I think I did the right thing. Nearly in tears for fear of doing something silly, "Read it again," I pleaded, "oh do read it to me again."

Obviously this was all right, for Yeats beamed, put on his pince nez attached to the broad black silk ribbon, and read through it again . . .

This time I was able to stutter: "Wonderful. Thank you so much. Wonderful. I must go and wash my hair," and crashed out.

Yeats's poem and Anne Gregory's response provide a welcome lighter moment in one of Yeats's densest volumes of verse. I turn now to the three alternate endings of the volume—the one that ends the main grouping of poems, then the one that ends the following separate sequence, "Words for Music Perhaps," and then the one that ends the final sequence, "A Woman Young and Old."

"Stream and Sun at Glendalough" concludes the main grouping of poems before the two sequences. As so often with Yeats's concluding lyrics, it contrasts images of perfection and even transcendence with more earthly conditions. We may wonder how the poem would be different if the title were "Stream and Sun at Rosses Point" or some other place, perhaps even "Miami Beach." The same issue arises with Wallace Stevens's title "The Idea of Order at Key West"—is there another one at Tampa, or on Cape Cod? In this case, set in a beautiful valley of the Wicklow Mountains, Glendalough is one of the most lovely and important ecclesiastical sites in Ireland. In a volume featuring self's debate with soul and transcendence of life versus immersion in it, knowing that Glendalough is an ecclesiastical site takes the poem out of a purely natural

realm and relocates it in Yeats's favorite position between
the ideal and the actual, as in so many poems from
"To the Rose upon the Rood of Time" onward. Hence
the first stanza pertains not only to nature but also to
its opposite, what "Coole Park, 1929" called "nature's
spite" and "Byzantium" called "images." The first line
of the second stanza uses a religious word, "repentance,"
to signal a turn away from a beautiful or ideal world and
back toward the speaker's heart, almost always in Yeats
the source of continued song. Correspondingly, after the
descriptive assertions of the opening stanza, the second
and third consist wholly of questions, not statements.
They show an attractive humility not always associated
with Yeats or his speakers:

> Repentance keeps my heart impure;
> But what am I that dare
> Fancy that I can
> Better conduct myself or have more
> Sense than a common man?
>
> What motion of the sun or stream
> Or eyelid shot the gleam
> That pierced my body through?
> What made me live like these that seem
> Self-born, born anew?

The poem's second stanza displays a speaker castigating
himself for delusions of grandeur, a lifelong danger for
Yeats. The final one begins with a rephrasing of Words-
worth's romantic pondering of whether the eye and ear

"half create" or "half perceive" in "Tintern Abbey"—
the speaker wonders whether the gleam that pierced his
body through originated in nature (the "sun or stream")
or himself (the "eyelid"). The remaining lines invoke
images that run throughout not just this volume but
Yeats's collected poetry as a whole. For instance, the idea
of a body pierced by a gleam of light appears in "The
Cold Heaven" from the *Responsibilities* volume, where
the speaker is "riddled with light," again in "The Mother
of God" from *The Winding Stair* with the "fallen flare /
Through the hollow of an ear," and the line "Another star
has shot an ear" from "A Nativity" in *Last Poems*. Simi-
larly, the "self-born, born anew" images of the final two
lines echo the "self-born" presences or images that mock
"man's enterprise" in "Among School Children" and the
"self-sown, self-begotten shape" in the gymnasts' gar-
den of "Colonus' Praise" from the *Tower* volume, and
above all "Those images that yet / Fresh images beget"
of "Byzantium" elsewhere in this one. That was one of
the many ways in which Yeats designed not just individ-
ual volumes of poems but his collected poems as a whole.
He liked, too, to end poems and sometimes bigger units
with questions rather than with answers, as though to
instigate the continuation of writing in his next volume.
We might call that form of closure really "anticlosure,"
since it holds things open rather than shuts them off.
Yeats did that for a number of his major lyrics, includ-
ing "Among School Children" with its dancer and dance,
or "Leda and the Swan" with its dilemma about knowl-
edge and power.

Passing over the wonderful Crazy Jane poems, based

on an actual old woman called Cracked Mary who lived near Yeats's tower and Lady Gregory's Coole Park, I press on to the second ending of the volume, the final poem of the "Words for Music Perhaps" sequence. Entitled "The Delphic Oracle upon Plotinus," its two five-line stanzas depict the Delphic Oracle's answer to the question of what happened to the third-century Neoplatonic philosopher Plotinus after his death:

> Behold that great Plotinus swim
> Buffeted by such seas;
> Bland Rhadamanthus beckons him,
> But the Golden Race looks dim,
> Salt blood blocks his eyes.
>
> Scattered on the level grass
> Or winding through the grove
> Plato there and Minos pass,
> There stately Pythagoras
> And all the choir of Love.

Yeats stays close here to the wording of his source, a translation by Stephen MacKenna, himself a friend of Synge, John O'Leary, Maud Gonne, and Yeats himself. It reads in part: "where Minos and Rhadamanthus dwell, great brethren of the golden race of mighty Zeus, where dwells the just Aeacus, and Plato, consecrated power, and stately Pythagoras, and all the choir of Immortal Love." But Yeats does not show Plotinus actually in the paradise, but only *swimming* there through the seas of life. The salt blood of life blocks his vision, but the immortals send an intense shaft of light so that he can *see* the vision even while immersed in the distractions of life. Yeats would later treat the same scene more satirically in the lyric "News for the Delphic Oracle," from *Last Poems,* where the "golden race" have become "golden codgers" instead and everybody lies around "sighing" in the Neoplatonic paradise while vitality lives on in the sensual and sexual world of Pan. But here Yeats treats the myth respectfully and admires the struggle of Plotinus to maintain glimpses of the eternal in the seas of transitory nature. Significantly, Yeats includes a date for this poem, 1931, just as he had for "Sun and Stream at Glendalough," which he dated 1932, as though to stress yet again that the poems in this volume do not appear in chronological order but in a different one.

Yeats had not finished his series of conclusions with "The Delphic Oracle upon Plotinus" but instead bestowed that honor on the final poem of the sequence, "A Woman Young and Old." "From the 'Antigone,'" as we have seen, occupies some of the same working manuscript pages as the very first poem of the entire collection, "In Memory of Eva Gore-Booth and Con Markiewicz." It helps to remember the story of Sophocles' tragedy *Antigone,* last of his Oresteia trilogy, in which after Oedipus' tragic exile from Thebes his sons Eteocles and Polyneices fall into civil war in which both die over the kingship. When the new king, Creon, refuses to bury Polyneices, his sister Antigone does so instead, for which Creon condemns her to death by burial alive in a cave. Yeats's poem adapts a chorus about Antigone's forthcoming death. Here is the poem, the last one in the vol-

ume. The quatrain structure of its sixteen lines would
have come across more regularly had Yeats's friend and
former secretary Ezra Pound not persuaded him to relo-
cate in typescript the original eighth line, "Inhabitant
of the soft cheek of a girl," to the second line, thus dis-
rupting the intended *abab* rhyme scheme:

> Overcome—O bitter sweetness,
> Inhabitant of the soft cheek of a girl—
> The rich man and his affairs,
> The fat flocks and the fields' fatness,
> Mariners, rough harvesters;
> Overcome Gods upon Parnassus;
>
> Overcome the Empyrean; hurl
> Heaven and Earth out of their places,
> That in the same calamity
> Brother and brother, friend and friend,
> Family and family,
> City and city may contend,
> By that great glory driven wild.
>
> Pray I will and sing I must,
> And yet I weep—Oedipus' child
> Descends into the loveless dust.

In the Greek play, the chorus intends these lines to cri-
tique the disruptive power of love to destabilize social,
religious, and moral hierarchies, whereas Yeats clearly
praises Antigone's action and approves of it. We may ask,
why does Yeats criticize the political commitments of the

Gore-Booth sisters at the beginning but praise those of Antigone at the end? After all, they both give their lives to political causes. Surely the answer has something to do with what "Coole and Ballylee, 1931" called "traditional sanctity and loveliness." Antigone upholds those traditional and cultural values, whereas in Yeats's view the Gore-Booth sisters betray them. In that way, Antigone stands with Lady Gregory's devotion to the values of Coole, in contrast to Eva and Con's abandonment of the similar ones of Lissadell. That becomes especially pertinent when we recall that Antigone's Greece had just passed through a civil war, as had Coole, Lissadell, and the rest of Ireland only a few years before Yeats wrote his poem. He takes his stand with the concrete and imaginative rather than the abstract and mechanical, and ends the volume with a particular image of a particular young woman.

But not altogether. As so often (think of the poem "Politics" at the end of the *Collected Poems*), Yeats ends with his own relation as poet to such matters, and with his own compulsion for continued speech. Separated by a space break on the page from the first line of its own quatrain, the concluding three lines ("Pray I will . . .") become a tercet on the poet's situation.

Note the sequencing of the three verbs describing the poet's action. First, he will pray, in accord with the values of traditional sanctity. Second, he then sings, or continues to be a poet. Yet even while doing so, he weeps at the tragedy of life. This is a different sort of ending from those images in "All Souls' Night" that conclude the *Tower* volume. Here, as in "The Circus Animals' Desertion," the poet plunges back into the human heart again, where all the ladders start. In a final turn, the poet then leaves us with the image not of himself but of Antigone, as she courageously descends to meet her fate. And that finally is what Yeats gives us, and what *The Winding Stair and Other Poems* gives us—the impetus to go on and to go forward, in his poetry and in our own lives. It is an ending that defies closure, as Yeats at his best so often does.

7. Sturge Moore's Jacket and Cover Design for
*The Winding Stair and other Poems*.

# THE WINDING STAIR
# AND OTHER POEMS

MACMILLAN AND CO., Limited
LONDON · BOMBAY · CALCUTTA · MADRAS
MELBOURNE

THE MACMILLAN COMPANY
NEW YORK · BOSTON · CHICAGO
DALLAS · ATLANTA · SAN FRANCISCO

THE MACMILLAN COMPANY
OF CANADA, LIMITED
TORONTO

# THE
# WINDING STAIR

## AND OTHER POEMS

BY

W. B. YEATS

MACMILLAN AND CO., LIMITED
ST. MARTIN'S STREET, LONDON

1933

**COPYRIGHT**

TO

## EDMUND DULAC

DEAR DULAC,

I saw my *Hawk's Well* played by students of our Schools of Dancing and of Acting a couple of years ago in a beautiful little theatre called ' The Peacock', which shares a roof with the Abbey Theatre. Watching Cuchulain in his lovely mask and costume, that old masked man who seems hundreds of years old, that Guardian of the Well, with your great golden wings and dancing to your music, I had one of those moments of excitement that are the dramatist's reward and decided there and then to dedicate to you my next book of verse.

' A Woman Young and Old ' was written before the publication of *The Tower*, but left out for some reason I cannot recall. I think that I was roused to write ' Death ' and ' Blood and the Moon ' by the assassination of Kevin O'Higgins, the finest intellect in Irish public life, and, I think I may add, to some extent, my friend. ' A Dialogue of Self and Soul ' was written in the spring of 1928 during a long illness, indeed finished the day before a Cannes doctor told me to stop writing. Then in the spring of 1929 life returned as an impression of the uncontrollable energy and daring of the great creators ; it seemed that but for journalism and criticism, all that evasion and explanation, the world would be torn in pieces. I wrote ' Mad as the Mist and Snow ', a mechanical little song, and after that almost all that group of poems called in memory of those exultant weeks ' Words for Music Perhaps '. Then ill again, I warmed myself back into life with ' Byzantium ' and ' Veronica's Napkin ', looking for a theme that might befit my years. Since then I have added a few poems to ' Words for Music Perhaps ', but always keeping the mood and plan of the first poems.

W. B. YEATS

1933

# CONTENTS

# CONTENTS

# CONTENTS

# IN MEMORY OF EVA GORE-BOOTH AND CON MARKIEWICZ

THE light of evening, Lissadell,
Great windows open to the south,
Two girls in silk kimonos, both
Beautiful, one a gazelle.
But a raving autumn shears
Blossom from the summer's wreath ;
The older is condemned to death,
Pardoned, drags out lonely years
Conspiring among the ignorant.
I know not what the younger dreams—
Some vague Utopia—and she seems,
When withered old and skeleton-gaunt,
An image of such politics.
Many a time I think to seek
One or the other out and speak
Of that old Georgian mansion, mix

Pictures of the mind, recall
That table and the talk of youth,
Two girls in silk kimonos, both
Beautiful, one a gazelle.

Dear shadows, now you know it all,
All the folly of a fight
With a common wrong or right.
The innocent and the beautiful
Have no enemy but time ;
Arise and bid me strike a match
And strike another till time catch ;
Should the conflagration climb,
Run till all the sages know.
We the great gazebo built,
They convicted us of guilt ;
Bid me strike a match and blow.

*October* 1927

# DEATH

Nor dread nor hope attend
A dying animal ;
A man awaits his end
Dreading and hoping all ;
Many times he died,
Many times rose again.
A great man in his pride
Confronting murderous men
Casts derision upon
Supersession of breath ;
He knows death to the bone—
Man has created death.

# A DIALOGUE OF SELF AND SOUL

## I

*My Soul*. I summon to the winding
    ancient stair ;
Set all your mind upon the steep
    ascent,
Upon the broken, crumbling battle-
    ment,
Upon the breathless starlit air,
Upon the star that marks the hidden
    pole ;
Fix every wandering thought upon
That quarter where all thought is
    done :
Who can distinguish darkness from
    the soul ?

4

*My Self.* The consecrated blade upon
    my knees
  Is Sato's ancient blade, still as it was,
  Still razor-keen, still like a looking-
    glass
  Unspotted by the centuries ;
  That flowering, silken, old embroid-
    ery, torn
  From some court-lady's dress and
    round
  The wooden scabbard bound and
    wound,
  Can, tattered, still protect, faded
    adorn.

*My Soul.* Why should the imagination
    of a man
  Long past his prime remember things
    that are
  Emblematical of love and war ?
  Think of ancestral night that can,
  If but imagination scorn the earth
  And intellect its wandering

To this and that and t'other thing,
Deliver from the crime of death and
    birth.

*My Self.* Montashigi, third of his
    family, fashioned it
Five hundred years ago, about it lie
Flowers from I know not what em-
    broidery—
Heart's purple—and all these I set
For emblems of the day against the
    tower
Emblematical of the night,
And claim as by a soldier's right
A charter to commit the crime once
    more.

*My Soul.* Such fullness in that quarter
    overflows
And falls into the basin of the mind
That man is stricken deaf and dumb
    and blind,
For intellect no longer knows

*Is* from the *Ought*, or *Knower* from
the *Known*—
That is to say, ascends to Heaven ;
Only the dead can be forgiven ;
But when I think of that my tongue's
a stone.

## II

*My Self*. A living man is blind and
drinks his drop.
What matter if the ditches are im-
pure ?
What matter if I live it all once more ?
Endure that toil of growing up ;
The ignominy of boyhood ; the dis-
tress
Of boyhood changing into man ;
The unfinished man and his pain
Brought face to face with his own
clumsiness ;

The finished man among his ene-
mies ?—

How in the name of Heaven can he
    escape
That defiling and disfigured shape
The mirror of malicious eyes
Casts upon his eyes until at last
He thinks that shape must be his
    shape ?
And what's the good of an escape
If honour find him in the wintry
    blast ?

I am content to live it all again
And yet again, if it be life to
    pitch
Into the frog-spawn of a blind man's
    ditch,
A blind man battering blind men ;
Or into that most fecund ditch of
    all,
The folly that man does
Or must suffer, if he woos
A proud woman not kindred of his
    soul.

I am content to follow to its source
Every event in action or in thought;
Measure the lot; forgive myself the
    lot!
When such as I cast out remorse
So great a sweetness flows into the
    breast
We must laugh and we must sing,
We are blest by everything,
Everything we look upon is blest.

# BLOOD AND THE MOON

## I

BLESSED be this place,
More blessed still this tower ;
A bloody, arrogant power
Rose out of the race
Uttering, mastering it,
Rose like these walls from these
Storm-beaten cottages—
In mockery I have set
A powerful emblem up,
And sing it rhyme upon rhyme
In mockery of a time
Half dead at the top.

## II

Alexandria's was a beacon tower, and
     Babylon's

10

An image of the moving heavens, a log-
　　book of the sun's journey and the
　　moon's ;
And Shelley had his towers, thought's
　　crowned powers he called them
　　once.


I declare this tower is my symbol ; I
　　declare
This winding, gyring, spiring tread-
　　mill of a stair is my ancestral
　　stair ;
That Goldsmith and the Dean, Berke-
　　ley and Burke have travelled there.


Swift beating on his breast in sibylline
　　frenzy blind
Because the heart in his blood-sodden
　　breast had dragged him down into
　　mankind,
Goldsmith deliberately sipping at the
　　honey-pot of his mind,

And haughtier-headed Burke that
    proved the State a tree,
That this unconquerable labyrinth of
    the birds, century after century,
Cast but dead leaves to mathematical
    equality ;

And God-appointed Berkeley that
    proved all things a dream,
That this pragmatical, preposterous
    pig of a world, its farrow that so
    solid seem,
Must vanish on the instant if the mind
    but change its theme ;

*Saeva Indignatio* and the labourer's
    hire,
The strength that gives our blood and
    state magnanimity of its own
    desire ;
Everything that is not God consumed
    with intellectual fire.

### III

The purity of the unclouded moon
Has flung its arrowy shaft upon the
  floor.
Seven centuries have passed and it is
  pure ;
The blood of innocence has left no
  stain.
There, on blood-saturated ground, have
  stood
Soldier, assassin, executioner,
Whether for daily pittance or in blind
  fear
Or out of abstract hatred, and shed
  blood,
But could not cast a single jet thereon.
Odour of blood on the ancestral
  stair !
And we that have shed none must
  gather there
And clamour in drunken frenzy for
  the moon.

## IV

Upon the dusty, glittering windows
    cling,
And seem to cling upon the moonlit
    skies,
Tortoiseshell butterflies, peacock but-
    terflies :
A couple of night-moths are on the
    wing.
Is every modern nation like the tower,
Half dead at the top ? No matter
    what I said,
For wisdom is the property of the dead,
A something incompatible with life ;
    and power,
Like everything that has the stain of
    blood,
A property of the living ; but no stain
Can come upon the visage of the moon
When it has looked in glory from a
    cloud.

# OIL AND BLOOD

In tombs of gold and lapis lazuli
Bodies of holy men and women exude
Miraculous oil, odour of violet.

But under heavy loads of trampled
    clay
Lie bodies of the vampires full of
    blood ;
Their shrouds are bloody and their lips
    are wet.

# VERONICA'S NAPKIN

THE Heavenly Circuit; Berenice's
    Hair;
Tent-pole of Eden; the tent's drapery;
Symbolical glory of the earth and air!
The Father and His angelic hierarchy
That made the magnitude and glory
    there
Stood in the circuit of a needle's eye.

Some found a different pole, and where
    it stood
A pattern on a napkin dipped in blood.

# SYMBOLS

A STORM-BEATEN old watch-tower,
A blind hermit rings the hour.

All-destroying sword-blade still
Carried by the wandering fool.

Gold-sewn silk on the sword-blade,
Beauty and fool together laid.

## SPILT MILK

WE that have done and thought,
That have thought and done,
Must ramble, and thin out
Like milk spilt on a stone.

# THE NINETEENTH CENTURY AND AFTER

Though the great song return no more
There's keen delight in what we have :
The rattle of pebbles on the shore
Under the receding wave.

## STATISTICS

' THOSE Platonists are a curse,' he said,
' God's fire upon the wane,
A diagram hung there instead,
More women born than men.'

# THREE MOVEMENTS

SHAKESPEAREAN fish swam the sea, far
    away from land ;
Romantic fish swam in nets coming to
    the hand ;
What are all those fish that lie gasping
    on the strand ?

# THE SEVEN SAGES

*The First.* My great-grandfather spoke
   to Edmund Burke
 In Grattan's house.

*The Second.*        My great-grand-
   father shared
 A pot-house bench with Oliver Gold-
   smith once.

*The Third.* My great - grandfather's
   father talked of music,
 Drank tar-water with the Bishop of
   Cloyne.

*The Fourth.* But mine saw Stella once.

*The Fifth.* Whence came our thought ?

*The Sixth.* From four great minds that
   hated Whiggery.

*The Fifth.* Burke was a Whig.

*The Sixth.*  Whether they knew or not,
  Goldsmith and Burke, Swift and the
      Bishop of Cloyne
  All hated Whiggery ; but what is
    Whiggery ?
  A levelling, rancorous, rational sort
    of mind
  That never looked out of the eye of
    a saint
  Or out of drunkard's eye.

*The Seventh.*        All's Whiggery now,
  But we old men are massed against
    the world.

*The First.* American colonies, Ireland,
    France and India
  Harried, and Burke's great melody
    against it.

*The Second.* Oliver Goldsmith sang
    what he had seen,
  Roads full of beggars, cattle in the
    fields,

But never saw the trefoil stained
  with blood,
The avenging leaf those fields raised
  up against it.

*The Fourth.* The tomb of Swift wears
  it away.

*The Third.*          A voice
Soft as the rustle of a reed from
  Cloyne
That gathers volume ; now a thun-
  der-clap.

*The Sixth.* What schooling had these
  four ?

*The Seventh.*   They walked the roads
Mimicking what they heard, as chil-
  dren mimic ;
They understood that wisdom comes
  of beggary.

# THE CRAZED MOON

CRAZED through much child-bearing
The moon is staggering in the sky ;
Moon-struck by the despairing
Glances of her wandering eye
We grope, and grope in vain,
For children born of her pain.

Children dazed or dead !
When she in all her virginal pride
First trod on the mountain's head
What stir ran through the countryside
Where every foot obeyed her glance !
What manhood led the dance !

Fly-catchers of the moon,
Our hands are blenched, our fingers
    seem

But slender needles of bone ;
Blenched by that malicious dream
They are spread wide that each
May rend what comes in reach.

## COOLE PARK, 1929

I MEDITATE upon a swallow's flight,
Upon an aged woman and her house,
A sycamore and lime tree lost in night
Although that western cloud is lumin-
    ous,
Great works constructed there in
    nature's spite
For scholars and for poets after us,
Thoughts long knitted into a single
    thought,
A dance-like glory that those walls
    begot.

There Hyde before he had beaten into
    prose
That noble blade the Muses buckled on,
There one that ruffled in a manly
    pose

For all his timid heart, there that slow
    man,
That meditative man, John Synge, and
    those
Impetuous men, Shaw Taylor and
    Hugh Lane,
Found pride established in humility,
A scene well set and excellent company.


They came like swallows and like
    swallows went,
And yet a woman's powerful character
Could keep a swallow to its first intent;
And half a dozen in formation there,
That seemed to whirl upon a compass-
    point,
Found certainty upon the dreaming
    air,
The intellectual sweetness of those
    lines
That cut through time or cross it
    withershins.

Here, traveller, scholar, poet, take your
    stand
When all those rooms and passages are
    gone,
When nettles wave upon a shapeless
    mound
And saplings root among the broken
    stone,
And dedicate—eyes bent upon the
    ground,
Back turned upon the brightness of
    the sun
And all the sensuality of the shade—
A moment's memory to that laurelled
    head.

## COOLE AND BALLYLEE,
### 1931

UNDER my window-ledge the waters
    race,
Otters below and moor-hens on the top,
Run for a mile undimmed in Heaven's
    face
Then darkening through ' dark ' Raft-
    ery's ' cellar ' drop,
Run underground, rise in a rocky place
In Coole demesne, and there to finish up
Spread to a lake and drop into a hole.
What's water but the generated soul ?

Upon the border of that lake's a wood
Now all dry sticks under a wintry sun,
And in a copse of beeches there I stood,
For Nature's pulled her tragic buskin
    on

And all the rant's a mirror of my mood:
At sudden thunder of the mounting
     swan
I turned about and looked where
     branches break
The glittering reaches of the flooded
     lake.

Another emblem there ! That stormy
     white
But seems a concentration of the sky ;
And, like the soul, it sails into the sight
And in the morning's gone, no man
     knows why ;
And is so lovely that it sets to right
What knowledge or its lack had set
     awry,
So arrogantly pure, a child might think
It can be murdered with a spot of ink.

Sound of a stick upon the floor, a sound
From somebody that toils from chair
          to chair ;

Beloved books that famous hands have
    bound,
Old marble heads, old pictures every-
    where ;
Great rooms where travelled men and
    children found
Content or joy ; a last inheritor
Where none has reigned that lacked a
    name and fame
Or out of folly into folly came.

A spot whereon the founders lived and
    died
Seemed once more dear than life ;
    ancestral trees
Or gardens rich in memory glorified
Marriages, alliances and families,
And every bride's ambition satisfied.
Where fashion or mere fantasy decrees
Man shifts about—all that great glory
    spent—
Like some poor Arab tribesman and
    his tent.

We were the last romantics—chose for
    theme
Traditional sanctity and loveliness ;
Whatever's written in what poets name
The book of the people ; whatever
    most can bless
The mind of man or elevate a rhyme ;
But all is changed, that high horse
    riderless,
Though mounted in that saddle Homer
    rode
Where the swan drifts upon a darken-
    ing flood.

## FOR ANNE GREGORY

'NEVER shall a young man,
Thrown into despair
By those great honey-coloured
Ramparts at your ear,
Love you for yourself alone
And not your yellow hair.'

'But I can get a hair-dye
And set such colour there,
Brown, or black, or carrot,
That young men in despair
May love me for myself alone
And not my yellow hair.'

'I heard an old religious man
But yesternight declare

That he had found a text to prove
That only God, my dear,
Could love you for yourself alone
And not your yellow hair.'

## SWIFT'S EPITAPH

SWIFT has sailed into his rest ;
Savage indignation there
Cannot lacerate his breast.
Imitate him if you dare,
World-besotted traveller ; he
Served human liberty.

## AT ALGECIRAS—A MEDITATION
## UPON DEATH

THE heron-billed pale cattle-birds
That feed on some foul parasite
Of the Moroccan flocks and herds
Cross the narrow Straits to light
In  the  rich  midnight  of  the  garden
    trees
Till  the  dawn  break  upon  those
    mingled seas.

Often at evening when a boy
Would I carry to a friend—
Hoping more substantial joy
Did an older mind commend—
Not such as are in Newton's metaphor,
But  actual  shells  of  Rosses'  level
    shore.

Greater glory in the sun,
An evening chill upon the air,
Bid imagination run
Much on the Great Questioner ;
What He can question, what if ques-
    tioned I
Can with a fitting confidence reply.

*November* 1928

# THE CHOICE

THE intellect of man is forced to choose
Perfection of the life, or of the work,
And if it take the second must refuse
A heavenly mansion, raging in the dark.
When all that story's finished, what's
    the news ?
In luck or out the toil has left its mark :
That old perplexity an empty purse,
Or the day's vanity, the night's re-
    morse.

# MOHINI CHATTERJEE

I ASKED if I should pray,
But the Brahmin said,
' Pray for nothing, say
Every night in bed,
" I have been a king,
I have been a slave,
Nor is there anything,
Fool, rascal, knave,
That I have not been,
And yet upon my breast
A myriad heads have lain." '

That he might set at rest
A boy's turbulent days
Mohini Chatterjee
Spoke these, or words like these.
I add in commentary,

' Old lovers yet may have
All that time denied—
Grave is heaped on grave
That they be satisfied—
Over the blackened earth
The old troops parade,
Birth is heaped on birth
That such cannonade
May thunder time away,
Birth-hour and death-hour meet,
Or, as great sages say,
Men dance on deathless feet.'

1928

# BYZANTIUM

THE unpurged images of day recede ;
The Emperor's drunken soldiery are
     abed ;
Night resonance recedes, night-walkers'
     song
After great cathedral gong ;
A starlit or a moonlit dome disdains
All that man is,
All mere complexities,
The fury and the mire of human veins.

Before me floats an image, man or
     shade,
Shade more than man, more image
     than a shade ;
For Hades' bobbin bound in mummy-
     cloth
May unwind the winding path ;

A mouth that has no moisture and no
    breath
Breathless mouths may summon ;
I hail the superhuman ;
I call it death-in-life and life-in-death.

Miracle, bird or golden handiwork,
More miracle than bird or handi-
    work,
Planted on the starlit golden bough,
Can like the cocks of Hades crow,
Or, by the moon embittered, scorn
    aloud
In glory of changeless metal
Common bird or petal
And all complexities of mire or
    blood.

At midnight on the Emperor's pave-
    ment flit
Flames that no faggot feeds, nor steel
    has lit,
Nor storm disturbs, flames begotten of
    flame,

Where blood-begotten spirits come
And all complexities of fury leave,
Dying into a dance,
An agony of trance,
An agony of flame that cannot singe a
    sleeve.

Astraddle on the dolphin's mire and
    blood,
Spirit after spirit ! The smithies break
    the flood,
The golden smithies of the Emperor !
Marbles of the dancing floor
Break bitter furies of complexity,
Those images that yet
Fresh images beget,
That dolphin-torn, that gong-tormented
    sea.

1930

# THE MOTHER OF GOD

THE three-fold terror of love ; a
    fallen flare
Through the hollow of an ear ;
Wings beating about the room ;
The terror of all terrors that I bore
The Heavens in my womb.

Had I not found content among the
    shows
Every common woman knows,
Chimney corner, garden walk,
Or rocky cistern where we tread the
    clothes
And gather all the talk ?

What is this flesh I purchased with my
    pains,

This fallen star my milk sustains,
This love that makes my heart's blood
    stop
Or strikes a sudden chill into my bones
And bids my hair stand up ?

# VACILLATION

## I

BETWEEN extremities
Man runs his course ;
A brand, or flaming breath,
Comes to destroy
All those antinomies
Of day and night ;
The body calls it death,
The heart remorse.
But if these be right
What is joy ?

## II

A tree there is that from its topmost
    bough
Is half all glittering flame and half all
    green

Abounding foliage moistened with the
    dew ;
And half is half and yet is all the scene ;
And half and half consume what they
    renew,
And he that Attis' image hangs be-
    tween
That staring fury and the blind lush
    leaf
May know not what he knows, but
    knows not grief.

### III

Get all the gold and silver that you can,
Satisfy ambition, or animate
The trivial days and ram them with
    the sun,
And yet upon these maxims meditate :
All women dote upon an idle man
Although their children need a rich
    estate ;
No man has ever lived that had enough
Of children's gratitude or woman's love.

No longer in Lethean foliage caught
Begin the preparation for your death
And from the fortieth winter by that
    thought
Test every work of intellect or faith
And everything that your own hands
    have wrought,
And call those works extravagance of
    breath
That are not suited for such men as
    come
Proud, open-eyed and laughing to the
    tomb.

## IV

My fiftieth year had come and gone,
I sat, a solitary man,
In a crowded London shop,
An open book and empty cup
On the marble table-top.

While on the shop and street I gazed
My body of a sudden blazed ;

E

And twenty minutes more or less
It seemed, so great my happiness,
That I was blessèd and could bless.

**v**

Although the summer sunlight gild
Cloudy leafage of the sky,
Or wintry moonlight sink the field
In storm-scattered intricacy,
I cannot look thereon,
Responsibility so weighs me down.

Things said or done long years ago,
Or things I did not do or say
But thought that I might say or do,
Weigh me down, and not a day
But something is recalled,
My conscience or my vanity appalled.

**VI**

A rivery field spread out below,
An odour of the new-mown hay

In his nostrils, the great lord of
    Chou
Cried, casting off the mountain snow,
' Let all things pass away.'

Wheels by milk-white asses drawn
Where Babylon or Nineveh
Rose ; some conqueror drew rein
And cried to battle-weary men,
' Let all things pass away.'

From man's blood-sodden heart are
    sprung
Those branches of the night and day
Where the gaudy moon is hung.
What's the meaning of all song ?
' Let all things pass away.'

## VII

*The Soul.* Seek out reality, leave things
    that seem.

*The Heart.* What, be a singer born and
    lack a theme ?

*The Soul.* Isaiah's coal, what more can
    man desire ?

*The Heart.* Struck dumb in the sim-
    plicity of fire !

*The Soul.* Look on that fire, salvation
    walks within.

*The Heart.* What theme had Homer
    but original sin ?

### VIII

Must we part, Von Hügel, though much
    alike, for we
Accept the miracles of the saints and
    honour sanctity ?
The body of Saint Teresa lies un-
    decayed in tomb,
Bathed in miraculous oil, sweet odours
    from it come,
Healing from its lettered slab.   Those
    self-same hands perchance
Eternalised the body of a modern saint
    that once

Had scooped out Pharaoh's mummy.
   I—though heart might find relief
Did I become a Christian man and
   choose for my belief
What seems most welcome in the tomb
   —play a predestined part.
Homer is my example and his un-
   christened heart.
The lion and the honeycomb, what has
   Scripture said ?
So get you gone, Von Hügel, though
   with blessings on your head.

   1932

## QUARREL IN OLD AGE

WHERE had her sweetness gone ?
What fanatics invent
In this blind bitter town,
Fantasy or incident
Not worth thinking of,
Put her in a rage.
I had forgiven enough
That had forgiven old age.

All lives that has lived ;
So much is certain ;
Old sages were not deceived :
Somewhere beyond the curtain
Of distorting days
Lives that lonely thing
That shone before these eyes
Targeted, trod like Spring.

# THE RESULTS OF THOUGHT

Acquaintance ; companion ;
One dear brilliant woman ;
The best-endowed, the elect,
All by their youth undone,
All, all, by that inhuman
Bitter glory wrecked.

But I have straightened out
Ruin, wreck and wrack ;
I toiled long years and at length
Came to so deep a thought
I can summon back
All their wholesome strength.

What images are these
That turn dull-eyed away,

Or shift Time's filthy load,
Straighten aged knees,
Hesitate or stay ?
What heads shake or nod ?

*August* 1981

# GRATITUDE TO THE UNKNOWN INSTRUCTORS

WHAT they undertook to do
They brought to pass ;
All things hang like a drop of dew
Upon a blade of grass.

# REMORSE FOR INTEMPERATE
# SPEECH

I RANTED to the knave and fool,
But outgrew that school,
Would transform the part,
Fit audience found, but cannot rule
My fanatic [1] heart.

I sought my betters : though in
 each
Fine manners, liberal speech,
Turn hatred into sport,
Nothing said or done can reach
My fanatic heart.

---

[1] I pronounce 'fanatic' in what is, I suppose,
the older and more Irish way, so that the last line
of each stanza contains but two beats.

Out of Ireland have we come.
Great hatred, little room,
Maimed us at the start.
I carry from my mother's womb
A fanatic heart.

*August* 28, 1931

## STREAM AND SUN AT GLENDALOUGH

THROUGH intricate motions ran
Stream and gliding sun
And all my heart seemed gay :
Some stupid thing that I had done
Made my attention stray.

Repentance keeps my heart impure ;
But what am I that dare
Fancy that I can
Better conduct myself or have more
Sense than a common man ?

What motion of the sun or stream
Or eyelid shot the gleam

That pierced my body through ?
What made me live like these that
    seem
Self-born, born anew ?

*June* 1982

# WORDS FOR MUSIC PERHAPS

## I

### CRAZY JANE AND THE BISHOP

BRING me to the blasted oak
That I, midnight upon the stroke,
(*All find safety in the tomb.*)
May call down curses on his head
Because of my dear Jack that's dead.
Coxcomb was the least he said :
*The solid man and the coxcomb.*

Nor was he Bishop when his ban
Banished Jack the Journeyman,
(*All find safety in the tomb.*)
Nor so much as parish priest,
Yet he, an old book in his fist,
Cried that we lived like beast and beast:
*The solid man and the coxcomb.*

The Bishop has a skin, God knows,
Wrinkled like the foot of a goose,
(*All find safety in the tomb.*)
Nor can he hide in holy black
The heron's hunch upon his back,
But a birch-tree stood my Jack :
*The solid man and the coxcomb.*

Jack had my virginity,
And bids me to the oak, for he
(*All find safety in the tomb.*)
Wanders out into the night
And there is shelter under it,
But should that other come, I spit :
*The solid man and the coxcomb.*

II

CRAZY JANE REPROVED

I care not what the sailors say :
All those dreadful thunder-stones,
All that storm that blots the day
Can but show that Heaven yawns ;

Great Europa played the fool
That changed a lover for a bull.
*Fol de rol, fol de rol.*

To round that shell's elaborate whorl,
Adorning every secret track
With the delicate mother-of-pearl,
Made the joints of Heaven crack :
So never hang your heart upon
A roaring, ranting journeyman.
*Fol de rol, fol de rol.*

### III

#### CRAZY JANE ON THE DAY OF JUDGMENT

' Love is all
Unsatisfied
That cannot take the whole
Body and soul ' ;
*And that is what Jane said.*

' Take the sour
If you take me,

I can scoff and lour
And scold for an hour.'
'*That's certainly the case,*' *said he.*

' Naked I lay,
The grass my bed ;
Naked and hidden away,
That black day ' ;
*And that is what Jane said.*

' What can be shown ?
What true love be ?
All could be known or shown
If Time were but gone.'
'*That's certainly the case,*' *said he.*


IV

CRAZY JANE AND JACK THE
JOURNEYMAN

I know, although when looks meet
I tremble to the bone,

F

The more I leave the door unlatched
The sooner love is gone,
For love is but a skein unwound
Between the dark and dawn.

A lonely ghost the ghost is
That to God shall come ;
I—love's skein upon the ground,
My body in the tomb—
Shall leap into the light lost
In my mother's womb.

But were I left to lie alone
In an empty bed,
The skein so bound us ghost to ghost
When he turned his head
Passing on the road that night,
Mine would walk being dead.

## V

### CRAZY JANE ON GOD

That lover of a night
Came when he would,

Went in the dawning light
Whether I would or no ;
Men come, men go :
*All things remain in God.*

Banners choke the sky ;
Men-at-arms tread ;
Armoured horses neigh
Where the great battle was
In the narrow pass :
*All things remain in God.*

Before their eyes a house
That from childhood stood
Uninhabited, ruinous,
Suddenly lit up
From door to top :
*All things remain in God.*

I had wild Jack for a lover ;
Though like a road
That men pass over
My body makes no moan

But sings on :
*All things remain in God.*


**VI**

CRAZY JANE TALKS WITH THE BISHOP

I met the Bishop on the road
And much said he and I.
' Those breasts are flat and fallen now,
Those veins must soon be dry ;
Live in a heavenly mansion,
Not in some foul sty.'

' Fair and foul are near of kin,
And fair needs foul,' I cried.
' My friends are gone, but that's a
    truth
Nor grave nor bed denied,
Learned in bodily lowliness
And in the heart's pride.

' A woman can be proud and stiff
When on love intent ;

But Love has pitched his mansion in
The place of excrement ;
For nothing can be sole or whole
That has not been rent.'


## VII

### CRAZY JANE GROWN OLD LOOKS
### AT THE DANCERS

I found that ivory image there
Dancing with her chosen youth,
But when he wound her coal-black
    hair
As though to strangle her, no scream
Or bodily movement did I dare,
Eyes under eyelids did so gleam :
*Love is like the lion's tooth.*


When she, and though some said she
    played
I said that she had danced heart's
    truth,

Drew a knife to strike him dead,
I could but leave him to his fate ;
For, no matter what is said,
They had all that had their hate :
*Love is like the lion's tooth.*

Did he die or did she die ?
Seemed to die or died they both ?
God be with the times when I
Cared not a thraneen for what chanced
So that I had the limbs to try
Such a dance as there was danced—
*Love is like the lion's tooth.*

## VIII

### GIRL'S SONG

I went out alone
To sing a song or two,
My fancy on a man,
And you know who.

Another came in sight
That on a stick relied
To hold himself upright :
I sat and cried.

And that was all my song—
When everything is told,
Saw I an old man young
Or young man old ?

IX

YOUNG MAN'S SONG

' She will change,' I cried,
' Into a withered crone.'
The heart in my side,
That so still had lain,
In noble rage replied
And beat upon the bone :

' Uplift those eyes and throw
Those glances unafraid :

She would as bravely show
Did all the fabric fade ;
No withered crone I saw
Before the world was made.'

Abashed by that report,
For the heart cannot lie,
I knelt in the dirt.
And all shall bend the knee
To my offended heart
Until it pardon me.


**X**

**HER ANXIETY**

Earth in beauty dressed
Awaits returning spring.
All true love must die,
Alter at the best
Into some lesser thing.
*Prove that I lie.*

Such body lovers have,
Such exacting breath,
That they touch or sigh.
Every touch they give,
Love is nearer death.
*Prove that I lie.*

### XI

#### HIS CONFIDENCE

Undying love to buy
I wrote upon
The corners of this eye
All wrongs done.
What payment were enough
For undying love ?

I broke my heart in two
So hard I struck.
What matter ? for I know
That out of rock,
Out of a desolate source,
Love leaps upon its course.

## XII

### LOVE'S LONELINESS

Old fathers, great-grandfathers,
Rise as kindred should.
If ever lover's loneliness
Came where you stood,
Pray that Heaven protect us
That protect your blood.

The mountain throws a shadow,
Thin is the moon's horn ;
What did we remember
Under the ragged thorn ?
Dread has followed longing,
And our hearts are torn.

## XIII

### HER DREAM

I dreamed as in my bed I lay,
All night's fathomless wisdom come,

That I had shorn my locks away
And laid them on Love's lettered tomb :
But something bore them out of sight
In a great tumult of the air,
And after nailed upon the night
Berenice's burning hair.

### XIV

#### HIS BARGAIN

Who talks of Plato's spindle ;
What set it whirling round ?
Eternity may dwindle,
Time is unwound,
Dan and Jerry Lout
Change their loves about.

However they may take it,
Before the thread began
I made, and may not break it
When the last thread has run,
A bargain with that hair
And all the windings there.

## XV

### THREE THINGS

' O  cruel  Death,  give  three  things
  back,'
*Sang a bone upon the shore ;*
' A child found all a child can lack,
Whether of pleasure or of rest,
Upon the abundance of my breast ' :
*A bone wave-whitened and dried in the*
  *wind.*

' Three dear things that women know,'
*Sang a bone upon the shore ;*
' A man if I but held him so
When my body was alive
Found all the pleasure that life gave ' :
*A bone wave-whitened and dried in the*
  *wind.*

' The third thing that I think of yet,'
*Sang a bone upon the shore,*
' Is that morning when I met

Face to face my rightful man
And did after stretch and yawn':
*A bone wave-whitened and dried in the*
    *wind.*

### XVI

#### LULLABY

Beloved, may your sleep be sound
That have found it where you fed.
What were all the world's alarms
To mighty Paris when he found
Sleep upon a golden bed
That first dawn in Helen's arms ?

Sleep, beloved, such a sleep
As did that wild Tristram know
When, the potion's work being done,
Roe could run or doe could leap
Under oak and beechen bough,
Roe could leap or doe could run ;

Such a sleep and sound as fell
Upon Eurotas' grassy bank

When the holy bird, that there
Accomplished his predestined will,
From the limbs of Leda sank
But not from her protecting care.

## XVII

### AFTER LONG SILENCE

Speech after long silence ; it is right,
All other lovers being estranged or
    dead,
Unfriendly lamplight hid under its
    shade,
The curtains drawn upon unfriendly
    night,
That we descant and yet again descant
Upon the supreme theme of Art and
    Song :
Bodily decrepitude is wisdom ; young
We loved each other and were ignorant.

## XVIII

### MAD AS THE MIST AND SNOW

Bolt and bar the shutter,
For the foul winds blow :
Our minds are at their best this night,
And I seem to know
That everything outside us is
*Mad as the mist and snow.*

Horace there by Homer stands,
Plato stands below,
And here is Tully's open page.
How many years ago
Were you and I unlettered lads
*Mad as the mist and snow ?*

You ask what makes me sigh, old
friend,
What makes me shudder so ?
I shudder and I sigh to think
That even Cicero
And many-minded Homer were
*Mad as the mist and snow.*

## XIX

### THOSE DANCING DAYS ARE GONE

Come, let me sing into your ear ;
Those dancing days are gone,
All that silk and satin gear ;
Crouch upon a stone,
Wrapping that foul body up
In as foul a rag :
*I carry the sun in a golden cup,*
*The moon in a silver bag.*

Curse as you may I sing it through ;
What matter if the knave
That the most could pleasure you,
The children that he gave,
Are somewhere sleeping like a top
Under a marble flag ?
*I carry the sun in a golden cup,*
*The moon in a silver bag.*

I thought it out this very day,
Noon upon the clock,

A man may put pretence away
Who leans upon a stick,
May sing, and sing until he drop,
Whether to maid or hag :
*I carry the sun in a golden cup,*
*The moon in a silver bag.*

## XX

### 'I AM OF IRELAND'

'*I am of Ireland,*
*And the Holy Land of Ireland,*
*And time runs on,' cried she.*
'*Come out of charity,*
*Come dance with me in Ireland.*'

One man, one man alone
In that outlandish gear,
One solitary man
Of all that rambled there
Had turned his stately head.
'That is a long way off,

G

And time runs on,' he said,
' And the night grows rough.'

' *I am of Ireland,*
*And the Holy Land of Ireland,*
*And time runs on,*' *cried she.*
' *Come out of charity*
*And dance with me in Ireland.*'

' The fiddlers are all thumbs,
Or the fiddle-string accursed,
The drums and the kettledrums
And the trumpets all are burst,
And the trombone,' cried he,
' The trumpet and trombone,'
And cocked a malicious eye,
' But time runs on, runs on.'

' *I am of Ireland,*
*And the Holy Land of Ireland,*
*And time runs on,*' *cried she.*
' *Come out of charity*
*And dance with me in Ireland.*'

## XXI

### THE DANCER AT CRUACHAN[1]
### AND CRO-PATRICK

I, proclaiming that there is
Among birds or beasts or men,
One that is perfect or at peace,
Danced on Cruachan's windy plain,
Upon Cro-Patrick sang aloud ;
All that could run or leap or swim
Whether in wood, water or cloud,
Acclaiming, proclaiming, declaiming
    Him.

[1] Pronounced in modern Gaelic as if spelt 'Crockan.'

## XXII

### TOM THE LUNATIC

Sang old Tom the lunatic
That sleeps under the canopy ;
' What change has put my thoughts
    astray
And eyes that had so keen a sight ?

What has turned to smoking wick
Nature's pure unchanging light ?

' Huddon and Duddon and Daniel
O'Leary,
Holy Joe, the beggar-man,
Wenching, drinking, still remain
Or sing a penance on the road ;
Something made these eyeballs weary
That blinked and saw them in a shroud.

' Whatever stands in field or flood,
Bird, beast, fish or man,
Mare or stallion, cock or hen,
Stands in God's unchanging eye
In all the vigour of its blood ;
In that faith I live or die.'

### XXIII

#### TOM AT CRUACHAN

On Cruachan's plain slept he
That must sing in a rhyme

What most could shake his soul :
' The stallion Eternity
Mounted the mare of Time,
'Gat the foal of the world.'

### XXIV

#### OLD TOM AGAIN

Things out of perfection sail,
And all their yellow canvas wear,
Nor shall the self-begotten fail
Though fantastic men suppose
Building-yard and stormy shore,
Winding-sheet and swaddling-clothes.

### XXV

#### THE DELPHIC ORACLE UPON PLOTINUS

Behold that great Plotinus swim
Buffeted by such seas ;
Bland Rhadamanthus beckons him,
But the Golden Race looks dim,
Salt blood blocks his eyes.

Scattered on the level grass
Or winding through the grove
Plato there and Minos pass,
There stately Pythagoras
And all the choir of Love.

*August* 19, 1931

# A WOMAN YOUNG AND OLD

## I

### FATHER AND CHILD

SHE hears me strike the board and say
That she is under ban
Of all good men and women,
Being mentioned with a man
That has the worst of all bad names;
And thereupon replies
That his hair is beautiful,
Cold as the March wind his eyes.

## II

### BEFORE THE WORLD WAS MADE

If I make the lashes dark
And the eyes more bright

And the lips more scarlet,
Or ask if all be right
From mirror after mirror,
No vanity's displayed :
I'm looking for the face I had
Before the world was made.

What if I look upon a man
As though on my beloved,
And my blood be cold the while
And my heart unmoved ?
Why should he think me cruel
Or that he is betrayed ?
I'd have him love the thing that was
Before the world was made.

### III

#### A FIRST CONFESSION

I admit the briar
Entangled in my hair
Did not injure me ;
My blenching and trembling

Nothing but dissembling,
Nothing but coquetry.

I long for truth, and yet
I cannot stay from that
My better self disowns,
For a man's attention
Brings such satisfaction
To the craving in my bones.

Brightness that I pull back
From the Zodiac,
Why those questioning eyes
That are fixed upon me?
What can they do but shun me
If empty night replies?

### IV

#### HER TRIUMPH

I did the dragon's will until you came
Because I had fancied love a casual
Improvisation, or a settled game

That followed if I let the kerchief fall :
Those deeds were best that gave the
    minute wings
And heavenly music if they gave it wit;
And then you stood among the dragon-
    rings.
I mocked, being crazy, but you mas-
    tered it
And broke the chain and set my ankles
    free,
Saint George or else a pagan Perseus ;
And now we stare astonished at the sea,
And a miraculous strange bird shrieks
    at us.

## V

### CONSOLATION

O but there is wisdom
In what the sages said ;
But stretch that body for a while
And lay down that head
Till I have told the sages
Where man is comforted.

How could passion run so deep
Had I never thought
That the crime of being born
Blackens all our lot?
But where the crime's committed
The crime can be forgot.

VI

CHOSEN

The lot of love is chosen.  I learnt that
    much
Struggling for an image on the track
Of the whirling Zodiac.
Scarce did he my body touch,
Scarce sank he from the west
Or found a subterranean rest
On the maternal midnight of my breast
Before I had marked him on his
    northern way,
And seemed to stand although in bed
    I lay.

I struggled with the horror of daybreak,
I chose it for my lot ! If questioned on
My utmost pleasure with a man
By some new-married bride, I take
That stillness for a theme
Where his heart my heart did seem
And both adrift on the miraculous
    stream
Where—wrote a learned astrologer—
The Zodiac is changed into a sphere.


## VII

### PARTING

*He.* Dear, I must be gone
    While night shuts the eyes
    Of the household spies ;
    That song announces dawn.

*She.* No, night's bird and love's
    Bids all true lovers rest,
    While his loud song reproves
    The murderous stealth of day.

*He.* Daylight already flies
  From mountain crest to crest.

*She.* That light is from the moon.

*He.* That bird . . .

*She.*                Let him sing on,
  I offer to love's play
  My dark declivities.

## VIII

### HER VISION IN THE WOOD

Dry timber under that rich foliage,
At wine-dark midnight in the sacred
    wood,
Too old for a man's love I stood in rage
Imagining men. Imagining that I
    could
A greater with a lesser pang assuage
Or but to find if withered vein ran
    blood,
I tore my body that its wine might
    cover
Whatever could recall the lip of lover.

And after that I held my fingers up,
Stared at the wine-dark nail, or dark
    that ran
Down every withered finger from the
    top ;
But the dark changed to red, and
    torches shone,
And deafening music shook the leaves ;
    a troop
Shouldered a litter with a wounded
    man,
Or smote upon the string and to the
    sound
Sang of the beast that gave the fatal
    wound.

All stately women moving to a song
With loosened hair or foreheads grief-
    distraught,
It seemed a Quattrocento painter's
    throng,
A thoughtless image of Mantegna's
    thought—

Why should they think that are for
    ever young ?
Till suddenly in grief's contagion
    caught,
I stared upon his blood-bedabbled
    breast
And sang my malediction with the rest.

That thing all blood and mire, that
    beast-torn wreck,
Half turned and fixed a glazing eye on
    mine,
And, though love's bitter-sweet had all
    come back,
Those bodies from a picture or a
    coin
Nor saw my body fall nor heard it
    shriek,
Nor knew, drunken with singing as
    with wine,
That they had brought no fabulous
    symbol there
But my heart's victim and its torturer.

### IX

#### A LAST CONFESSION

What lively lad most pleasured me
Of all that with me lay ?
I answer that I gave my soul
And loved in misery,
But had great pleasure with a lad
That I loved bodily.

Flinging from his arms I laughed
To think his passion such
He fancied that I gave a soul
Did but our bodies touch,
And laughed upon his breast to think
Beast gave beast as much.

I gave what other women gave
That stepped out of their clothes,
But when this soul, its body off,
Naked to naked goes,

He it has found shall find therein
What none other knows,

And give his own and take his own
And rule in his own right ;
And though it loved in misery
Close and cling so tight,
There's not a bird of day that dare
Extinguish that delight.


X

MEETING

Hidden by old age awhile
In masker's cloak and hood,
Each hating what the other loved,
Face to face we stood :
' That I have met with such,' said he,
' Bodes me little good.'

' Let others boast their fill,' said I,
' But never dare to boast
That such as I had such a man
For lover in the past ;

H

Say that of living men I hate
Such a man the most.'

'A loony'd boast of such a love,'
He in his rage declared :
But such as he for such as me—
Could we both discard
This beggarly habiliment—
Had found a sweeter word.

## XI

### FROM THE 'ANTIGONE'

Overcome—O bitter sweetness,
Inhabitant of the soft cheek of a girl—
The rich man and his affairs,
The fat flocks and the fields' fatness,
Mariners, rough harvesters ;
Overcome Gods upon Parnassus ;

Overcome the Empyrean ; hurl
Heaven and Earth out of their places,

That in the same calamity
Brother and brother, friend and friend,
Family and family,
City and city may contend,
By that great glory driven wild.

Pray I will and sing I must,
And yet I weep—Oedipus' child
Descends into the loveless dust.

# NOTES

'I AM of Ireland' is developed from three or four lines of an Irish fourteenth-century dance song somebody repeated to me a few years ago. 'The sun in a golden cup' in the poem that precedes it, though not 'The moon in a silver bag', is a quotation from somewhere in Mr. Ezra Pound's 'Cantos'. In this book and elsewhere, I have used towers, and one tower in particular, as symbols and have compared their winding stairs to the philosophical gyres, but it is hardly necessary to interpret what comes from the main track of thought and expression. Shelley uses towers constantly as symbols, and there are gyres in Swedenborg, and in Thomas Aquinas and certain classical authors. Part of the symbolism of 'Blood and the Moon' was suggested by the fact that Thoor Ballylee has a waste room at the top and that butterflies come in through the loopholes and die against the window-panes. The 'learned astrologer' in 'Chosen' was Macrobius, and the particular passage was found for me by Dr. Sturm, that too little known poet and mystic. It is from Macrobius's comment upon 'Scipio's Dream' (Lib. I. Cap. XII. Sec. 5): '... when the sun is in Aquarius, we sacrifice to the Shades, for it is in the sign inimical to human life; and from thence the meeting-place of Zodiac and Milky Way, the descending soul by its defluction is drawn out of the spherical, the sole divine form, into the cone'. In 'The Mother of God' the words 'a fallen flare through the hollow of an ear' are, I am told, obscure. I had in my memory Byzantine mosaic pictures of the Annunciation, which show a line drawn from a star to the ear of the Virgin. She conceived of the Word, and therefore through the ear a star fell and was born.

THE END

*Printed in Great Britain by* R. & R. CLARK, LIMITED, *Edinburgh.*

# NOTES

## DEDICATION

The French-born artist, musician, and designer Edmund Dulac (1882–1953) met Yeats shortly after moving to London in 1904 and became a lifelong friend. Known particularly for his book illustrations, Dulac contributed both book and theater designs for Yeats's work, such as the Japanese Noh-influenced *Four Plays for Dancers* (1921), which included the play *At the Hawk's Well,* in which the Irish hero Cuchulain seeks to drink from the water of immortality. Dulac had designed costumes, lighting, and a decorated cloth for the drama, as well as providing both music and masks along with playing the First Musician himself.

The Irish patriot and politician Kevin O'Higgins (1892–1927) served as vice-president, minister for economic affairs, and then minister for justice and external affairs in the first Irish Free State government. In apparent retaliation for die-hard Republican executions, he was assassinated on his way to Mass. Poems pertinent to him include "Death," "Blood and the Moon," and "Parnell's Funeral." In late 1927 and early 1928 Yeats suffered from congestion of the lungs accompanied by serious bleeding.

## IN MEMORY OF EVA GORE-BOOTH AND CON MARKIEWICZ

First published in *The Winding Stair* (New York: Fountain Press, 1929).

Constance Markiewicz (née Gore-Booth, 1868–1927) and

Eva Gore-Booth (1870–1926) were the two elder daughters of the Anglo-Irish landowning Gore-Booth family. Yeats first met them in 1894 and at one point thought of proposing to Eva.

1: Lissadell is the gray country mansion and former family seat of the Gore-Booths, a little outside the town of Sligo, where Yeats had many relatives on his mother's side of the family. It was built in 1832 in late Georgian style. 4: In a prose memoir Yeats compares Eva to a gazelle. 7f: Con Markiewicz was sentenced to death for her part in the Easter Rising of 1916 (she served as deputy leader of the rebel contingent at Stephen's Green in Dublin) but then reprieved; she remained active in hard-line Irish politics and worked among the poor in Dublin's slums. Eva engaged in political activity, too, particularly promoting women's rights and trade unions.

## DEATH

First published in *The Winding Stair* (New York: Fountain Press, 1929).

In the dedication to Dulac, Yeats said that he was roused to write both this poem and "Blood and the Moon" by the assassination of Kevin O'Higgins, "the finest intellect in Irish public life."

## A DIALOGUE OF SELF AND SOUL

First published in *The Winding Stair* (New York: Fountain Press, 1929).

While preparing the Fountain Press volume, Yeats told Olivia Shakespear in a letter from October 1927, "I am writing a new tower poem 'Sword and Tower,' which is a choice of rebirth rather than deliverance from birth. I make my Japanese sword and its silk covering my symbol of life" (*L* 729). The tower was his own summer residence at Ballylee for which he named the preceding volume, *The Tower* (1928). He utilized it in several poems, including "Blood and the Moon." The poem is written in eight-line stanzas, a unit favored by Yeats in his maturity but obscured for some readers by the frequent line turnovers of the display in this volume.

**10:** In 1920 his Japanese admirer Junzo Sato had presented Yeats with a ceremonial Japanese sword that had been in his family for more than five hundred years. **25:** The sword maker Bishu Osafune Motoshige (or Montashigi) worked in the town of Osafune in the early fifteenth century.

## BLOOD AND THE MOON

First published in *The Exile* (Spring 1928) and then in *The Winding Stair* (1929).

The poem begins with the speaker at Yeats's tower, Thoor Ballylee near Gort in Galway, which has cottages at its base. In his "Notes" to the volume, Yeats wrote, "Part of the symbolism of 'Blood and the Moon' was suggested by the fact that Thoor Ballylee has a waste room at the top and that butterflies come in through the loopholes and die against the window-panes."

**13–14:** The Pharos or lighthouse (ca. 280 B.C.) on the island of Pharos in the harbor at Alexandria was considered one of the Seven Wonders of the ancient world. The ancient Babylonians developed an advanced astronomy and astrology. **15–16:** Yeats wrote in his essay "Prometheus Unbound" that the English Romantic poet Percy Bysshe Shelley (1792–1822) "shaped my life" (*LE* 121–22). Shelley used the phrase "thought's crowned powers" in the ecstatic Chorus of Spirits in the fourth act of his visionary drama *Prometheus Unbound,* which in another essay Yeats called a "sacred book" (*EE* 51). **18f:** All born in Ireland, the writer Oliver Goldsmith (1728–74), the writer and from 1713 dean of St. Patrick's Cathedral in Dublin Jonathan Swift (1667–1745), the philosopher and bishop George Berkeley (1685–1753), and the politician, orator, and aesthetician Edmund Burke (1729–97) represented to Yeats Irish eighteenth-century civilization at its best. **28:** Yeats translated the Latin "Saeva Indignatio" as "savage indignation" in his version of "Swift's Epitaph" later in the present volume.

## OIL AND BLOOD

First published in *The Winding Stair* (New York: Fountain Press, 1929).

## VERONICA'S NAPKIN

First published in *Words for Music Perhaps and Other Poems* (Dublin: Cuala Press, 1932).

In Christian tradition, St. Veronica handed Jesus a cloth to wipe his face on his way to the crucifixion and received it back with his face imprinted upon it.

1: "The Heavenly Circuit" is the title of a section of the *Enneads* by the Neoplatonic philosopher Plotinus (A.D. 205–269/270) that describes God as the center of a perfect circle around which heavenly bodies rotate; so, metaphorically, do human souls. Yeats used Stephen MacKenna's 1921 translation of that work. Berenice II (ca. 273–221 B.C.) married Ptolemy III of Egypt in 247 and offered her hair for his safe return from war; in return he named a constellation after her tresses. 2: The "tent-pole of Eden" may be the North Star or axis of the earth. 7–8: The "different pole" is presumably the cross on which Jesus was crucified; the "pattern on a napkin" is his face imprinted upon Veronica's cloth.

## SYMBOLS

First published in *Words for Music Perhaps and Other Poems* (Dublin: Cuala Press, 1932) and in *The Spectator,* 2 December 1932.

## SPILT MILK

First published in *Words for Music Perhaps and Other Poems* (Dublin: Cuala Press, 1932).

## THE NINETEENTH CENTURY AND AFTER

First published in *Words for Music Perhaps and Other Poems* (Dublin: Cuala Press, 1932).

In a letter to Olivia Shakespear in March 1929 Yeats prefaced these lines with the comment "I have come to fear the world's last great poetical period is over" (*L* 759).

## STATISTICS

First published in *Words for Music Perhaps and Other Poems* (Dublin: Cuala Press, 1932).

Platonists are, of course, followers of the Greek philosopher Plato (ca. 429–347 B.C.). Yeats associated them with partisans of modern abstractions and statistics.

## THREE MOVEMENTS

First published in *Words for Music Perhaps and Other Poems* (Dublin: Cuala Press, 1932).

Yeats's prose draft of this poem reads "Passion in Shakespeare was a great fish in the sea, but from Goethe to the end of the Romantic movement the fish was in the net. It will soon be dead upon the shore."

## THE SEVEN SAGES

First published in *Words for Music Perhaps and Other Poems* (Dublin: Cuala Press, 1932).

For Burke, Goldsmith, Swift, and Berkeley ("the Bishop of Cloyne") see above, note to "Blood and the Moon," 18f.

2: Henry Grattan (1746–1820), Irish orator and Protestant M.P., championed both legislative independence and the rights of Catholics. He was the dominant figure in "Grattan's Parliament" ("Grattan's house" in the poem), which was dissolved by the Act of Union in 1800, after which he served as M.P. for Dublin, 1806–20. 6: Berkeley wrote a book advocating the medicinal properties of tar water, used thus by some Native Americans; his recipe favored pouring a gallon of water over a quart of tar and then stirring and draining. 7: "Stella" was Swift's name for Esther Johnson (d. 1728), his presumably Platonic lover; he published his letters to her in *Journal to Stella*. 9: the Whig party in English politics grew out of liberal aristocrats supporting the Protestant William III against the Catholic James II; Burke and Swift were originally Whigs before moving toward the Tories. Yeats associated Whiggery with leveling and materialism. 20: "Burke's great melody" would be his speeches and writings, in which a common theme is emancipation: the emancipation of the American colonies, of Irish trade and Catholics, of India from the rule of the East India Company, and of France from what he saw as the eventual tyranny of the French Revolution. 21: Goldsmith sang of rural poverty and depopulation in his famous poem "The Deserted Village." 23: Trefoil refers to three-leaved plants, of which the lesser yellow trefoil is also known as the shamrock.

## THE CRAZED MOON

First published in *Words for Music Perhaps and Other Poems* (Dublin: Cuala Press, 1932).

The poem draws upon Yeats's theories of phases of the moon as metaphor for psychological and historical phases in his book of esoteric philosophy *A Vision*, of which the first version appeared in 1925.

## COOLE PARK, 1929

First published in Lady Gregory, *Coole* (Dublin: Cuala Press, 1931), and then in *Words for Music Perhaps and Other Poems* (Dublin: Cuala Press, 1932).

Coole Park was the County Galway estate of Yeats's patron, friend, and collaborator the nationalist and author Lady Augusta Gregory (1852–1932). Forced by financial circumstances to sell it to the Forestry Commission, she remained on as tenant for the remaining five years of her life. Yeats's prose draft reads: "Describe house in first stanza. Here Synge came, Hugh Lane, Shaw Taylor [*sic*], many names. I too in my timid youth. Coming and going like migratory birds. Then address the swallows fluttering in their dream like circles. Speak of the rarity of the circumstances that bring together such concords of men. Each man more than himself through whom an unknown life speaks. A circle ever returning into itself."

9: Douglas Hyde (1860–1949), Irish poet and translator, was the first president of the Gaelic League and later of Ireland. Yeats thought that immersion in practical affairs had blunted his prose style. 11: The "one that ruffled in a manly pose" is likely Yeats himself. 13: John Synge (1871–1909), Irish playwright, poet, and translator, wrote the controversial masterpiece *Playboy of the Western World* and served as codirector of the Abbey Theatre along with Lady Gregory and Yeats himself. 14: John Shawe-Taylor (1866–1911) and Hugh Lane (1875–1915) were both nephews of Lady Gregory. After an early military career including service in the Boer War, Shawe-Taylor became a leader in Irish land reform; Lane was an art collector and critic who in a well-meaning but controversial move offered his impressive collection to the Dublin Corporation if it would build an art gallery to house it.

## COOLE AND BALLYLEE, 1931

First published in *Words for Music Perhaps and Other Poems* (Dublin: Cuala Press, 1932).

Yeats's Thoor Ballylee stands near Lady Gregory's Coole Park in County Galway; he bought the tower partly to have a home base nearby. Yeats liked to imagine that the stream flowing past his tower ended up in Coole Lake via an underground passage.

**4:** The Gaelic poet Anthony Rafferty (1784–1835) was blind, hence Yeats's word "dark" for him. Rafferty wrote often of the region, and Yeats particularly liked to invoke his praise of the young beauty Mary Hynes. One of his lines declares, "There is a strong cellar in Ballylee." **26:** The "somebody" would be Lady Gregory herself, then in steep decline. **44:** "the book of the people" is a phrase used by Rafferty that Yeats quoted in *Explorations*, 215. **47:** Yeats invoked the ancient Greek poet Homer several times in his poetry, including another linkage with Rafferty in section II of "The Tower."

## FOR ANNE GREGORY

First published in *Words for Music Perhaps and Other Poems* (Dublin: Cuala Press, 1932) and in *The Spectator*, 2 December 1932.

Anne Gregory (1911–2008) was the daughter of Robert Gregory and granddaughter of Lady Gregory. She has an ironic account of Yeats composing and then reading her the poem in her brief memoir *Me and Nu: Childhood at Coole*.

## SWIFT'S EPITAPH

First published in *The Dublin Magazine*, October–December 1931 and then in *Words for Music Perhaps and Other Poems* (Dublin: Cuala Press, 1932).

The poem is a close adaptation of the Latin epithet composed for himself by Jonathan Swift (1667–1745), whom Yeats also invokes in "Blood and the Moon" and "The Seven Sages." Swift's tomb is in St. Patrick's Cathedral, Dublin.

## AT ALGECIRAS—A MEDITATION UPON DEATH

First published in *A Packet for Ezra Pound* (Dublin: Cuala Press, 1929) and, after two magazine printings, in *Words for Music Perhaps and Other Poems* (Dublin: Cuala Press, 1932).

Algeciras is a city in southern Spain, near Gibraltar, where Yeats recuperated from lung congestion in late 1928.

3–6: Morocco is on the northern coast of Africa, across the Strait of Gibraltar from Algeciras. The "mingled seas" are the Mediterranean Sea and the Atlantic Ocean. 11: The English scientist Sir Isaac Newton (1642–1727) once wrote, "I do not know how I may appear to the world; but to myself I seem to have been only like a boy, playing on the seashore, and diverting myself in now and then finding another pebble or prettier shell than ordinary, while the great ocean of truth lay all undiscovered before me." 12: Rosses is a wide beach near Sligo familiar to Yeats from his childhood days; he also mentions it in his early poem "The Stolen Child."

## THE CHOICE

First published as the next to last stanza of "Coole and Ballylee, 1931" in *Words for Music Perhaps and Other Poems* (Dublin: Cuala Press, 1932).

## MOHINI CHATTERJEE

First published in *A Packet for Ezra Pound* (Dublin: Cuala Press, 1929) and, after two magazine printings, in *Words for Music Perhaps and Other Poems* (Dublin: Cuala Press, 1932). It was a companion poem to "At Algeciras."

Yeats met the Bengali Brahmin sage Mohini Chatterjee

(1858–1936) when he came to lecture to the Hermetic Society
in Dublin in 1885–86.


## BYZANTIUM

First published in *Words for Music Perhaps and Other Poems*
(Dublin: Cuala Press, 1932).

The late Roman emperor Constantine rebuilt the ancient
city of Byzantium as Constantinople, which became the cap-
ital of first the entire Roman Empire and then of the East-
ern Roman Empire. Its modern name is Istanbul, in Turkey.
Yeats's prose draft read: "Describe Byzantium as it is in the
system towards the end of the first Christian millennium. A
walking mummy. Flames at the street corners, where the soul
is purified, birds of hammered gold singing in the golden trees,
in the harbour [dolphins] offering their backs to the wailing
dead that they may carry them to paradise."

In a well-known passage from *A Vision*, Yeats wrote: "I
think if I could be given a month of Antiquity and leave to
spend it where I chose, I would spend it in Byzantium a little
before Justinian opened St. Sophia and closed the Academy of
Plato. . . . I think that in early Byzantium, and maybe never
before or since in recorded history, religious, aesthetic, and
practical life were one, that architect and artificers . . . spoke
to the multitude and the few alike."

**5:** The dome is probably that of Santa Sophia or Hagia
Sophia (Holy Wisdom), the famous church constructed by the
emperor Justinian in sixth-century Byzantium. **11:** In Greek
mythology Hades is lord of the underworld, where the shades
of the dead congregate. **16:** The Romantic poet Coleridge used
the phrase "The Nightmare Life-in-Death" in "The Rime of
the Ancient Mariner."

## THE MOTHER OF GOD

First published in *Words for Music Perhaps and Other Poems* (Dublin: Cuala Press, 1932).

In his concluding "Notes" to this volume, Yeats writes: "In 'The Mother of God' the words 'a fallen flare through the hollow of an ear" are, I am told, obscure. I had in my memory Byzantine mosaic pictures of the Annunciation, which show a line drawn from a star to the ear of the Virgin. She conceived of the Word, and therefore through the ear a star fell and was born."

## VACILLATION

First published in *Words for Music Perhaps and Other Poems* (Dublin: Cuala Press, 1932). There each section had its own subtitle and the later sections II and III were combined: I, What is Joy; II (including the current II and III), The Burning Tree; III, Happiness; IV, Conscience; V, Conquerors; VI, A Dialogue; VII, Von Hügel.

**11–12:** The tree that is half flame and half green comes from the medieval Welsh collection of tales *The Mabinogion*. Yeats quoted the relevant passage in his early essay "The Celtic Element in Literature" as translated by Lady Charlotte Guest: ". . . beautiful passage about the burning Tree, that has half its beauty from calling up a fancy of leaves so living and beautiful, they can be of no less living and beautiful a thing than flame: 'They saw a tall tree by the side of the river, one half of which was in flames from the root to the top, and the other half was green and in full leaf'" (*EE* 130). **16f:** Attis is a vegetation god in Greek mythology who castrated himself when driven to frenzy by Cybele the earth goddess and was turned into a pine tree. In the procession at Attis' festival, the priest would hang his image on a sacred pine tree. **27:** In Greek mythology Lethe was one of the rivers of Hades; drinking its waters made souls forget the past. **59:** "The great lord of Chou" is presumably

Chou-kung, who died in 1105 B.C. and was known as the Duke of Chou. He was a Chinese statesman and author who advised his brother in overthrowing the Shang dynasty; Confucius later cited him as a model minister. **63:** Famous for its astronomy and astrology among other arts and sciences, Babylon was the chief city of ancient Mesopotamia; Nineveh was the capital of the ancient Assyrian empire, destroyed by Babylonians and Medes in 612 B.C. **74:** In the Bible (Isaiah 6) an angel touches Isaiah's lips with a live coal to purify him and enable him to become a prophet. **77:** Yeats followed Lady Gregory in seeing ancient poets, whether Irish or Greek, as singing what from a Christian perspective would be our fallen world. Yeats remembered in his introduction to *The Oxford Book of Modern Verse* Lady Gregory telling him that she preferred poems translated from the Irish by Frank O'Connor because "they come out of original sin." **78:** Baron Friedrich von Hügel (1852–1925), the son of an Austrian diplomat father and Scots mother, became a Catholic religious philosopher of mystical bent. Yeats read his *The Mystical Element of Religion, as Studied in St. Catherine of Genoa and Her Friends*, 1908. **80:** Saint Teresa of Avila (1515–82) was a Spanish Carmelite nun and mystic. Yeats read the account of her allegedly undecayed body in Lady Lovat's *The Life of Saint Teresa*, 1911. **89:** In the Bible (Judges 14) Samson kills a lion and later takes honey from its carcass. He then makes the episode into a riddle, "Out of the eater came forth meat, and out of the strong came forth sweetness," and eventually tells his wife the answer, which she uses to betray him.

## QUARREL IN OLD AGE

First published in *Words for Music Perhaps and Other Poems* (Dublin: Cuala Press, 1932).

The poem likely grew out of a quarrel with Maud Gonne over a hunger strike by women prisoners. **16:** "targeted" here likely means carrying a round shield, or "targe."

## THE RESULTS OF THOUGHT

First published in *Words for Music Perhaps and Other Poems* (Dublin: Cuala Press, 1932).

The "companion" is likely Olivia Shakespear and the "one dear brilliant woman" Lady Gregory.

## GRATITUDE TO THE UNKNOWN INSTRUCTORS

First published in *Words for Music Perhaps and Other Poems* (Dublin: Cuala Press, 1932).

The "Unknown Instructors" are the spirits who inspired the automatic writing that led to Yeats's book of esoteric philosophy, psychology, and history *A Vision*, first published in 1925.

## REMORSE FOR INTEMPERATE SPEECH

First published in *Words for Music Perhaps and Other Poems* (Dublin: Cuala Press, 1932).

## STREAM AND SUN AT GLENDALOUGH

First published in *Words for Music Perhaps and Other Poems* (Dublin: Cuala Press, 1932).

Glendalough (Irish for "The Valley of the Two Lakes") is a beautiful area in the Wicklow Mountains containing an extensive monastic site known especially for its round tower.

## WORDS FOR MUSIC PERHAPS

With one exception, all the poems in this sequence were published under the general title "Words for Music Perhaps" in *Words for Music Perhaps and Other Poems* (Dublin: Cuala Press, 1932), though Yeats lightly revised the order. He added the one exception, poem VI ("Crazy Jane Talks with the Bishop"), for *The Winding Stair and Other Poems* (London: Macmillan, 1933). I have indicated place of first publication for only those poems in the sequence first published elsewhere.

As Yeats explained in the introductory letter to Edmund Dulac, he was recovering from a long illness and "in the spring of 1929 life returned as an impression of the uncontrollable energy and daring of the great creators . . . I wrote 'Mad as the Mist and Snow,' a mechanical little song, and after that almost all that group of poems called in memory of those exultant weeks 'Words for Music Perhaps.'" He told Olivia Shakespear that the title meant "not so much that they may be sung as that I may define their kind of emotion to myself. I want them to be all emotion and all impersonal"; and again that "'For Music' is only a name, nobody will sing them'" (*L* 758, 769).

## I. CRAZY JANE AND THE BISHOP

First published in *The London Mercury*, November 1930, and *The New Republic*, 12 November 1930.

Yeats wrote to Olivia Shakespear in November 1931 that he based Crazy Jane on an old woman called Cracked Mary "who lives in a cottage near Gort—She has just sent Lady Gregory some flowers in spite of the season and [has] an amazing power of audacious speech. One of her great performances is a description of how the meanness of a Gort shopkeeper's wife over the price of a glass of porter made her so despair of the human race that she got drunk" (*L* 785–86).

9: Yeats first used "Jack the Journeyman" as a name in a song from his play *The Pot of Broth*, 1903, and in a note also attributed it to Cracked Mary.

## II. CRAZY JANE REPROVED

First published in *The London Mercury*, November 1930, and in *The New Republic*, 12 November 1930.

**5–6:** In Greek mythology the god Zeus assumes the form of a bull to carry off the Phoenician princess Europa to Crete.

## III. CRAZY JANE ON THE DAY OF JUDGMENT

In Christian doctrine Judgment Day comes as part of the apocalypse at the end of time, when good and evil are judged and sent to Heaven or Hell.

## VI. CRAZY JANE TALKS WITH THE BISHOP

This poem was not part of the original *Words for Music Perhaps*. Yeats added it for *The Winding Stair and Other Poems*, 1933. Yeats does not often pun in his poetry, but does so here in line 17.

## VII. CRAZY JANE GROWN OLD LOOKS AT THE DANCERS

First published in *The London Mercury,* November 1930, and *The New Republic,* 12 November 1930.

**18:** Thraneen is the Irish word for a blade of grass or straw.

## VIII. GIRL'S SONG

First published in *The New Republic,* 22 October 1930.

## IX. YOUNG MAN'S SONG

First published in *The New Republic,* 22 October 1930.

## X. HER ANXIETY

First published in *The New Republic,* 22 October 1930.

## XI. HIS CONFIDENCE

First published in *The New Republic*, 22 October 1930.

## XII. LOVE'S LONELINESS

First published in *The New Republic*, 22 October 1930.

## XIII. HER DREAM

First published in *The New Republic*, 22 October 1930.
    8: For Berenice's hair, see note to "Veronica's Napkin," line 1, above.

## XIV. HIS BARGAIN

First published in *The New Republic*, 22 October 1930.
    1: Glaucon discusses the "spindle of Necessity" in Book X of Plato's *Republic*. It resembles Yeats's gyres in some ways; Yeats's lover claims that his love will remain steadfast amid ongoing cyclical changes.

## XV. THREE THINGS

First published in *The New Republic*, 2 October 1929.

## XVI. LULLABY

First published in *The New Keepsake* (an anthology), London, 1931.
    4–6: In Greek mythology Paris, son of King Priam of Troy, runs away with the wife of King Menelaus, Helen, thus precipitating the Trojan War. 8: In medieval legend such as Malory's *Le Morte d'Arthur* the adulterous love of the Cornish knight Tristan and Irish princess Isolde causes them to betray King Mark. 14f: In Greek legend Zeus came to Leda, wife of the king

of Sparta, in the shape of a swan while she was bathing in the Eurotas river.

## XVII. AFTER LONG SILENCE

This poem grew out of Yeats's long relationship with Olivia Shakespear (1863–1938), his former lover and lifelong friend.

## XVIII. MAD AS THE MIST AND SNOW

7: Horace (65–8 B.C.) was a Roman poet and author of the *Ars Poetica* (*Art of Poetry*); Homer, of course, was the Greek epic poet regarded as creator of the *Iliad* and *Odyssey*. 8: Plato (ca. 429–347 B.C.) was the famous Greek philosopher and author of *The Republic* among other works. 9: Known in English as both Tully and Cicero, Marcus Tullius Cicero (106–43 B.C.) was a leading Roman politician and orator. 17: "many-minded" is a translation of "polymetis," Homer's word for Odysseus.

## XIX. THOSE DANCING DAYS ARE GONE

First published in *The London Mercury,* November 1930, and *The New Republic,* 12 November 1930.

7–8: Yeats indicates in his concluding note to this volume, "The sun in a golden cup . . . is a quotation from somewhere in Mr. Ezra Pound's 'Cantos.'" The phrase comes from Pound's Canto XXIII and in turn derives from a line in the Greek poet Stesichorus about a sunset; Yeats indicated elsewhere that silver and gold together are alchemical symbols of perfection.

## XX. "I AM OF IRELAND"

Yeats indicates in the concluding note to this volume, "'I am of Ireland' is developed from three or four lines of an Irish fourteenth-century dance song somebody repeated to me a

few years ago." The "somebody" was the younger Irish writer
Frank O'Connor.

## XXI. THE DANCER AT CRUACHAN
## AND CRO-PATRICK

Cruachan, in County Roscommon, is the ancient capital of
Connaught associated with Queen Maeve. Cro-Patrick (Pat-
rick's Mountain) in County Mayo is associated with St. Pat-
rick's banishing of snakes from Ireland and serves as a center
of Catholic pilgrimage.

## XXII. TOM THE LUNATIC

The name Tom the Lunatic probably derives from Tom of Bed-
lam, a term for inmates of the London lunatic asylum Bed-
lam. 7: Huddon, Duddon, and Daniel O'Leary are names from
an Irish folktale that Yeats included under the title "Donald
and His Neighbours" in *Fairy and Folk Tales of the Irish Peas-
antry* (1888). He used the names himself at the start of the
"Stories of Michael Robartes and His Friends" section of the
1937 edition of *A Vision*, where each stanza begins "Huddon,
Duddon, and Daniel O'Leary / Delighted me as a child." 8:
"Holy Joe" is probably not a specific person; the colloquial
term "holy Joe" refers to anyone especially or ostentatiously
pious, often with negative or satiric connotations.

## XXIII. TOM AT CRUACHAN

For Cruachan, see note to "The Dancer at Cruachan and Cro-
Patrick," above.

## XXIV. OLD TOM AGAIN

In a 1931 letter to his wife, Yeats called this poem "a reply to the Dancer's song," referring to "The Dancer at Cruachan and Cro-Patrick," above.

## XXV. THE DELPHIC ORACLE UPON PLOTINUS

The oracle of Apollo at Delphi was the best-known one in the Classical world. The poem adapts the oracle's response when asked about the fate of the Greek Neoplatonic philosopher Plotinus (A.D. 205–269/270) after death. Yeats's source was Stephen MacKenna's translation of *Plotinus: The Ethical Treatises* (London: Medici Society, 1917), which reads in part: "where Minos and Rhadamanthus dwell, great brethren of the golden race of mighty Zeus, where dwells the just Aeacus, and Plato, consecrated power, and stately Pythagoras, and all the choir of Immortal Love." Yeats treats the same subject more satirically in his "News for the Delphic Oracle" from *Last Poems,* where the "golden race" have become "golden codgers" instead.

3–4: In Greek mythology Rhadamanthus is one of the three main judges of souls in the paradisal Elysium which the good may attain after death. He and the other two main judges, Minos and Aeacus, are all sons of Zeus and thus members of the "Golden Race." 8: Plato (ca. 429–347 B.C.) is the famous Greek philosopher mentioned previously in the volume. 9: Pythagoras (ca. 582–507 B.C.) was a Greek philosopher who developed doctrines of the transmigration of souls and of the mathematical and musical basis of the world.

## A WOMAN YOUNG AND OLD

This sequence formed part of the original *The Winding Stair* volume (New York: Fountain Press, 1929), where it also concluded that book. All the poems first appeared there. To some extent the sequence balances "A Man Young and Old," the closing sequence of the preceding volume, *The Tower*.

## I. FATHER AND CHILD

Yeats's daughter, Anne, told me in conversation that this poem grew out of an actual incident in family life, when her father disapproved of a young man that she was seeing.

## III. A FIRST CONFESSION

14: The Zodiac, of course, is the significant band of the sky containing the stars and planets important in astrology. See also note to poem VI, "Chosen."

## IV. HER TRIUMPH

10: The killing of a dragon figures prominently in the story of the Greek mythological hero Perseus, who freed the princess Andromeda from its captivity, and of the Christian Saint George, who freed a Libyan princess about to be sacrificed to it.

## V. CONSOLATION

Yeats included both this poem and "A First Confession" in a 1927 letter to Olivia Shakespear in which he described this one as "not so innocent" (*L* 725).

## VI. CHOSEN

Yeats titled this poem "The Choice" in the original *Winding Stair* volume of 1929. He wrote in a note there, "I have symbolized a woman's love as the struggle of the darkness to keep the sun from rising from its earthy bed. In the last stanza of The Choice I change the symbol to that of the souls of man and woman ascending through the Zodiac." He deleted that passage but expanded another part of the notes to *The Winding Stair and Other Poems*, 1933; see note to line 17, below. Yeats wrote to the scholar H. J. C. Grierson in 1926 that he had been reading John Donne's "A Nocturnal upon St. Lucy's Day" and had "used the arrangement of the rhymes in the stanzas for a poem of my own," namely "Chosen."

17: Yeats wrote in the "Notes" that conclude the 1933 volume reproduced here that "The 'learned astrologer' in 'Chosen' was Macrobius, and the particular passage . . . is from Macrobius's comment upon 'Scipio's Dream'" (see his "Notes," above). He wrote there, too, that the spherical is "the sole divine form."

Ambrosius Macrobius (fl. A.D. 400) composed among other works a Neoplatonic commentary on Cicero's *Somnium Scipionis*.

## VIII. HER VISION IN THE WOOD

This poem draws on the legends of the Greek love story of Aphrodite and Adonis and of the Irish one of Diarmuid and Grania, in both of which the female mourns the slaying of her lover by a wild boar.

19: "Quattrocento" is the Italian term for the fifteenth century. 20: Andrea Mantegna (1431–1506) was an Italian Renaissance painter whose work often depicts violent scenes, sometimes from unusual perspectives.

## XI. FROM THE 'ANTIGONE'

The ancient Greek tragedy *Antigone* concludes the Oresteia trilogy by Sophocles (496–406 B.C.), in which after King Oedipus's fall and exile from Thebes his sons Eteocles and Polyneices fall into a civil war over the kingship that claims both their lives. When the new king, Creon, refuses to bury Polyneices, his sister Antigone does so instead, for which Creon condemns her to death by burial alive in a cave. Yeats's poem adapts a chorus about Antigone's forthcoming death. Yeats's friend and former secretary Ezra Pound persuaded him to relocate in typescript the original eighth line, "Inhabitant of the soft cheek of a girl," to the second line, thus disrupting the original *abab* rhyme scheme.

6: The mountain Parnassus, near Delphi, was sacred to the Muses in Greek mythology; one of its twin peaks is named for Apollo, the other for Dionysus. 7: The Empyrean is the highest sphere of the heavens in ancient cosmology and associated with fire. 10: "Brother and brother": Antigone's brothers, Eteocles and Polyneices, kill each other; see general note to poem, above. 15: "Oedipus' child" is Antigone, sister of Eteocles and Polyneices.

## [YEATS'S] NOTES

Yeats concluded *The Winding Stair and Other Poems* (1933) with a page and a half labeled "Notes." Those pertaining to specific poems are glossed under those poems. Information not included there will be found in the following paragraph.

The late medieval Irish poem reads: "Ich am of Irlonde, / And of the holy londe / Of Irlonde. / Goode sire, praye ich thee, / For of sainte charitee, / Com and dance with me / In Irlonde." Emanuel Swedenborg (1688–1772) was a Swedish scientist, mystic, and religious philosopher whose best-known work is *Heaven and Hell,* which influenced both Blake and Yeats, among other writers. The thirteenth-century Thomas Aquinas (1225–74) became one of the most influential of all Roman Catholic theologians. Dr. Frank Pearce Sturm (1879–1942) was a translator, poet, and mystic philosopher who practiced in Lancashire. Yeats discussed astrology and horoscopes with him and included one of his poems in *The Oxford Book of Modern Verse,* 1936.